KTAA 태권도 신품새 [한영판]

초판발행 / 2022년 9월 15일

개발자 / 지현철, 지수민
감수자 / 손천택
펴낸이 / 문상필
디자인 / 손인문

펴낸곳 / 상아기획
크기 / 4×6배판 무선제본
등록번호 / 제318-1997-000041호
주소 / 서울시 영등포구 경인로82길 3-4, 715호 (문래동1가, 센터플러스)
대표전화 / 02-2164-2700
홈페이지 / www.tkdsanga.com
이메일 / 0221642700@daum.net

ISBN / 979-11-86196-23-6　13690
가격 / 20,000원

저작권은 개발자에게 있습니다. 저자와 협의로 인지를 생략합니다.
* 잘못 만들어진 책은 구매하신 서점에서 교환해드립니다.

Printed in KOREA

KTAA 태권도
신 품 새

개 발   지현철 · 지수민
감 수   손천택

차 례

I. 신 품새의 개요 ········· 5
    1. 신 품새의 의미 ········· 7
    2. 신 품새 개발의 필요성 ········· 7
    3. 신 품새의 기대 효과 ········· 8
    4. 신 품새의 개발 원칙 ········· 9

II. 신 품새 ········· 11
    생태 품새 I : 노란 띠 과정 ········· 14
    생태 품새 II : 파란 띠 과정 ········· 20
    생태 품새 III : 빨간 띠 과정 ········· 26
    생태 품새 IV : 1단 과정 ········· 32
    생태 품새 V : 2단 과정 ········· 38
    생태 품새 VI : 3단 과정 ········· 44
    생태 품새 VII : 4단 과정 ········· 50

I. 신 품새의 개요

1. 신 품새의 의미

'신 품새'란 전통에 대비되는 개념으로 현대적, 또는 태권도 기술의 현실을 반영하여 새롭게 개발한 품새라는 뜻이다. 2018 아시안게임을 대비하여 개발한 품새가 기존 품새와 전혀 다른 의도와 목적을 가지고 개발한 '새 품새'라면, '신 품새'는 기존 품새의 개발 목적과 내용 체계를 존중하고 기존 품새의 정통성을 인정하는 가운데 태권도의 신기술을 반영한 '생활 태권도 적합 창작 품새'이다. 즉, '신 품새'는 공인 품새의 핵심 기술과 그동안 발전한 새로운 기술을 결합하고 도장 현실의 요구와 기대를 반영하여 새롭게 개발한 품새이다. 신 품새는 수련생에게 품새 수련 동기를 부여하고, 나아가 공인 품새를 더욱 적극적으로 수련하게 하는 데 중요한 의미를 두고 있다.

2. 신 품새 개발의 필요성

품새는 자신을 보호하거나 상대를 공격하는 데 필요한 무예 기술을 가상의 적을 상대로 혼자 연습하는 수련 틀이다. 그런데 문화가 발달하고 태권도가 발전하면서 품새를 수련하는 의도나 목적이 크게 달라지고 있다. 단순히 호신 능력을 기르거나 그에 따른 자신감을 얻는 차원을 넘어 인성 교육이나 심미적 가치를 표현하는 등의 다양한 목적으로 품새를 익히는 수련생이 늘어나고 있다.

나아가 태권도가 무예 스포츠로 재정립되어 올림픽의 핵심 스포츠로 발전하면서 경기화에 따른 다양한 발기술이 개발되고, 도장 활성화 방안으로 각종 품새 경연대회가 개최되는 과정을 통해서 품새가 아시안게임의 정식 종목으로 채택되자 국기원의 공인 품새로 수련생의 다양한 품새 수련 욕구를 충족시킬 수 없는 상황을 맞이하고 있다.

더군다나 최근 생활체육이 활성화되면서 태권도를 즐겁게 수련하며 건강을 증진하고 삶의 질적 향상을 꾀하려는 수련생이 전례 없이 늘어나고 있다. 하지만, 손기술 중심의 단조롭고 편향된 국기원 공인 품새가 수련생의 다양한 학습 욕구를 충족시키지 못해 새로운 품새 개발에 대한 도장의 요청이 점증하고 있다. 또한 손기술 위주의 편향된 기존 품새의 동작 구성은 도장 중심의 생활 태권도와 학교 중심의 전문 태권도의 분열을 심화, 고착시키고 있다.

따라서 대한생활태권도협회(이하 생태)는 태권도의 스포츠화, 태권도 품새의 경기화, 태권도 시범의 공연화 등을 통해 개발된 새로운 기술을 반영한 '신 품새'를 개발하여 수련생이 다양한 손발 기술이 결합 된 태권도 품새를 음악에 맞춰 즐겁게 수련함으로써 품새 수련 동기를 증진하고 태권도의 인성 교육적 목표, 건강 교육적 목표, 문화 예술적 목표 등을 보다 효과적으로 달성하고자 한다.

3. 신 품새의 기대 효과

쉬운 접근. '신 품새'를 개발하여 잘 활용하면 수련생이 태권도 및 태권도 품새에 좀 더 쉽게 접근하여 품새 수련의 즐거움을 맛볼 수 있다. '신 품새'는 그동안 개발된 다양한 태권도 기술을 적극적으로 수용하여 다채롭게 구성함으로써 수련생의 기대를 충실히 반영하고 있기 때문이다.

수련 욕구 자극. '신 품새'는 국기원 공인 품새의 단조로운 구성에 따른 지루함과 단련 중심의 품새 수련에서 벗어나 다양한 손발 기술을 음악에 맞춰 흥겹게 수련함으로써 품새 수련 욕구를 자극하여 각 단급에서 익혀야 할 주요 기술을 즐겁게 익힐 수 있는 장점이 있다.

디딤돌 역할. '신 품새'는 기존 품새의 핵심 기술에 새로운 기술을 가미하여 음악에 맞춰 재구성하였으므로 즐겁게 수련하면서 공인 품새의 핵심 기술을 쉽게 익힐 수 있을 뿐만 아니라 공인 품새의 수련을 회피하는 수련생이 '신 품새'를 디딤돌 삼아 공인 품새를 더욱 열심히 수련하게 하는 효과가 있다.

조화로운 수련. '신 품새'는 그동안 품새 중심의 도장 태권도와 겨루기 중심의 경기 태권도, 손기술 중심의 도장 태권도와 발차기 중심의 전문 태권도로 이원화된 태권도를 하나의 태권도로 통합하여 조화로운 태권도 수련을 가능케 함으로써 도장에서 전문 선수가 배출되는 효과를 가져올 수 있다.

기예적 표현력 향상. '신 품새'는 21세기 문화 복지 시대의 요구로 빠르게 발전하는 태권도 공연에 필요한 기본기술을 익혀 호신 능력의 향상, 건강의 증진, 인성의 함양 등의 가치를 실현하는 차원을 넘어 창조적인 예술 활동에 필요한 기예적 표현력을 길러주는 효과가 있다.

4. 신 품새의 개발 원칙

'신 품새'는 국기원 공인 품새의 미비점을 보완하여 품새 수련 동기를 부여하고 그에 따른 품새 수련 효과를 높이기 위해 다음과 같은 품새 개발 원칙을 정하고 세부 지침을 세워 개발하였다.

공인 품새의 의도를 반영한 품새 개발. '신 품새'는 국기원 공인 품새의 개발 의도와 기술의 발전 단계를 고려하여 난이도를 점진적으로 높여가는 방식으로 개발하였다. 생태 품새 I, II, III은 유급자 품새에 해당하므로 음양의 원리를 따르고 팔괘의 의미를 살려 개발하고, 생태 품새 IV, V, VI, VII은 고려, 금강, 태백, 평원 품새의 개발 의도와 연계하여 창의적으로 개발하였다.

공인 품새와 연계한 품새 개발. '신 품새'는 실전 공방을 전제하되 기예적 스포츠의 특성을 반영한 품새를 개발하였다. 태권도는 무예로서 급소를 효과적으로 타격하여 상대를 제압하는 격투 능력을 기를 수 있어야 할 뿐만 아니라 경기 태권도의 특성을 충실히 반영해야 한다. 따라서 그동안 경기·경연을 통해서 새로 개발된 다양한 기술을 품새 선에 충실히 배치하되 전통 품새의 의도를 크게 벗어나지 않는 범위에서 개발하였다.

태권도의 다양한 추구 가치를 구현하는 품새 개발. '신 품새'는 실전을 전제한 공방 기술뿐만 아니라 도장의 교육 태권도가 추구하는 건강 증진, 인성 함양, 감상 능력 배양 등의 가치를 구현할 수 있는 기술과 동작을 반영한 품새를 개발하였다. 특히, 태권도 수련생의 생활체육 의도와 잠재력 개발을 중요하게 생각하는 품새를 개발하였다. 즉, 전통 한복을 편하게 입을 수 있는 생활한복으로 제작하듯이 전통 품새의 미비점을 보완 현대화하여 생활태권도 품새로 개발하였다.

신 품새 개발 세부 지침

① 전통 태권도 기술을 인정하고 존중하는 생활 태권도 품새를 개발한다.
② 전통 품새에 반영되지 않은 주요 기술을 단계적으로 충실히 반영한다.
③ 경기 태권도, 품새 경연대회, 태권도 시범 또는 공연 등을 통해 개발된 다양한 신기술을 적극적으로 반영한다.
④ 호신 효과가 있지만 생활 태권도로도 가치 있는 기술과 동작을 적극적으로 반영한다.
⑤ 신체의 균형 발전을 위해 좌우 대칭의 원칙에 따라 기술이나 동작이 품새 선에 배치되도록 한다.
⑥ 손기술과 발기술이 균형 있게 반영되고 적합한 밟기 기술이 적절히 포함되도록 한다.
⑦ 8방향을 벗어나지 않는 품새 선에 필요 동작을 전후좌우 대칭 구조로 배치한다. 품새는 음양 사상에 따르며, 사상이 분화하여 팔괘로 나타나고, 팔괘는 철저한 대칭 구조를 갖기 때문이다.

Ⅱ. 신 품새

단급 분류	품새 명칭	품새 선	동작	품새 개발 의도
생태 품새 I	노란 띠 과정	ㅜ	35	얼굴, 몸통, 아래를 막고 지르고, 밟기로 이동하며 차는 기본기술을 익히는 가운데 기본의 중요성과 강유의 의미를 깨닫게 한다.
생태 품새 II	파란 띠 과정	ㅍ	44	다양한 복합 동작과 연결 동작을 완급을 조절하며 빠르고 힘있게 익히는 가운데 배움의 열정, 힘의 위엄 있는 표현, 그리고 고요한 위세의 의미를 깨닫게 한다.
생태 품새 III	빨간 띠 과정	┼	37	신체의 다양한 부위로 다양한 손발 기술을 밟기와 함께 유연하고 조화롭게 발휘하는 가운데 유연함, 웅장함, 그리고 성장의 의미를 깨닫게 한다.
생태 품새 IV	1단 과정	朩	35	손발의 특수 부위로 독특한 공방 기술을 다양하게 발휘하는 가운데 고려 건국의 패기와 고려인의 기개를 느끼는 동시에 '명분-지조-의리'의 선비 정신을 깨치도록 한다.
생태 품새 V	2단 과정	ㅎ	57	대칭 또는 비대칭으로 구성한 다양한 손발 기술을 완급 조절로 균형 있게 발휘하는 가운데 금강산의 정기를 느끼고 태권도인다움의 지智와 덕德을 깨닫게 한다.
생태 품새 VI	3단 과정	ㅜ	58	복합 동작을 중속도로 절제하여 온건하게 발휘하는 가운데 백두산의 정기를 느끼고, 단군의 높은 이상인 홍익인간을 실천하는 결의를 다지도록 한다.
생태 품새 VII	4단 과정	ㅍ	75	상호 모순되거나 배치되는 연계 동작을 유연하게 발휘하는 가운데 부드러움이 강함을 이긴다는 유능제강柔能制剛과 평온이 격정을 이긴다는 평화의 정신을 깨닫게 한다.

생태 품새 I : 노란 띠 과정

- 품새 선: ┷
- 권장 시간 : 50초
- 품새의 구성

  태극 1~2장의 핵심 기술인 앞서기, 아래막기, 몸통막기, 얼굴막기, 몸통지르기, 앞차기에 주춤서 몸통·얼굴 지르기, 내딛기, 물러딛기 딛기 등의 기술을 보강하여 초보 기술의 수련 범위를 확장하고, 겨루기 능력을 더욱 향상할 수 있도록 구성하였다.

16 신품새

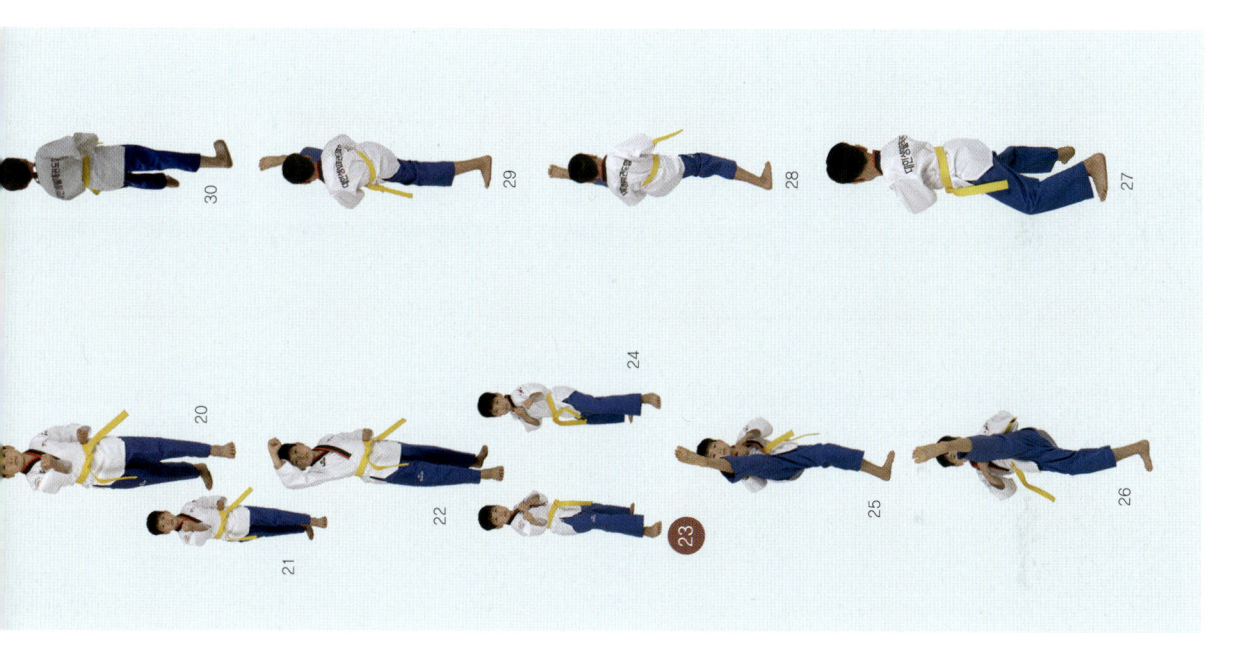

생태 품새 I : 노란 띠 과정　17

생태 품새 I 요약 설명

순서	시선	위치	서 기	동 작	품 명
준비	북	북	나란히 서기	한발 벌려	기본 준비서기
1	북	북	주춤 서기	양 주먹 당기며	주춤서기
2	북	북	주춤 서기	제자리	왼 몸통지르기
3	북	북	주춤 서기	제자리	오른 몸통지르기
4	북	북	주춤 서기	제자리	몸통-몸통-얼굴 연속지르기
5	북	북	주춤 서기	제자리	몸통-몸통-얼굴 연속지르기
6	북	북	주춤 서기	제자리	왼 얼굴 지르기
7	북	북	나란히 서기	한발 당겨	나란히 서기
8	서	서	왼 앞서기	왼발 옮겨 내어	오른 몸통 안막기
9	서	서	오른 앞서기	오른발 내딛어	왼 몸통 지르기
10	동	동	오른 앞서기	오른발 돌아 옮겨 딛어	왼 몸통 안막기
11	동	동	왼 앞서기	왼발 내딛어	오른 몸통 지르기
12	북	북	왼 앞굽이	왼발 옮겨딛어 내려막고	오른 몸통 지르기
13	북	북	오른 앞굽이	오른발 내딛어	몸통지르기(기합)
14	서	서	왼 앞서기	왼발 옮겨딛어	왼 내려막기
15-16	서	서	오른 앞굽이	오른 앞차고 내딛어	오른 얼굴 지르기
17	동	동	오른 앞서기	오른발 돌아 옮겨딛어	오른 내려막기
18-19	동	동	왼 앞굽이	왼 앞차고 내딛어	왼 얼굴 지르기
20	북	북	왼 앞서기	왼발 옮겨딛어	오른 몸통 안막기
21	북	북	왼 앞서기	제자리	오른 몸통 안막기(4초)
22	북	북	오른 앞서기	오른발 내딛어	오른 얼굴 막기(4초)
23	북	북	겨룸새	왼발 물러딛어	겨룸새(기합)
24	북	북	겨룸새	발바꿔 딛기-두번 제자리 딛기	겨룸새
25-26	북	북	겨룸새	오른 앞차고	왼 앞차기

27	남	남	겨룸새	돌아 딛고	겨룸새
28-29	남	남	겨룸새	왼 앞차고	오른 앞차기
30-31	남	남	왼 앞굽이	왼발 내딛어 내려막고	오른 몸통 지르기
32	남	남	오른 앞굽이	오른발 내딛어	오른 몸통지르기(기합)
바로	북	북	나란히 서기	왼발 돌아딛어	기본 준비 서기

생태 품새 Ⅱ : 파란 띠 과정

- 품새 선: ㅗ
- 권장 시간 : 55초
- 품새의 구성

태극 3~4장의 간단한 막기 기술과 4~5장의 치기 기술에 다양한 막기 기술을 결합하고, 앞차기, 돌려차기, 옆차기와 내딛기, 물러딛기, 돌아딛기 등과 연계하여 기본적인 공방 기술을 심화 발전시키고 겨루기 능력을 촉진하는 동시에 등척성 운동을 도입하여 기술의 자각적 이해력을 향상하도록 구성하였다.

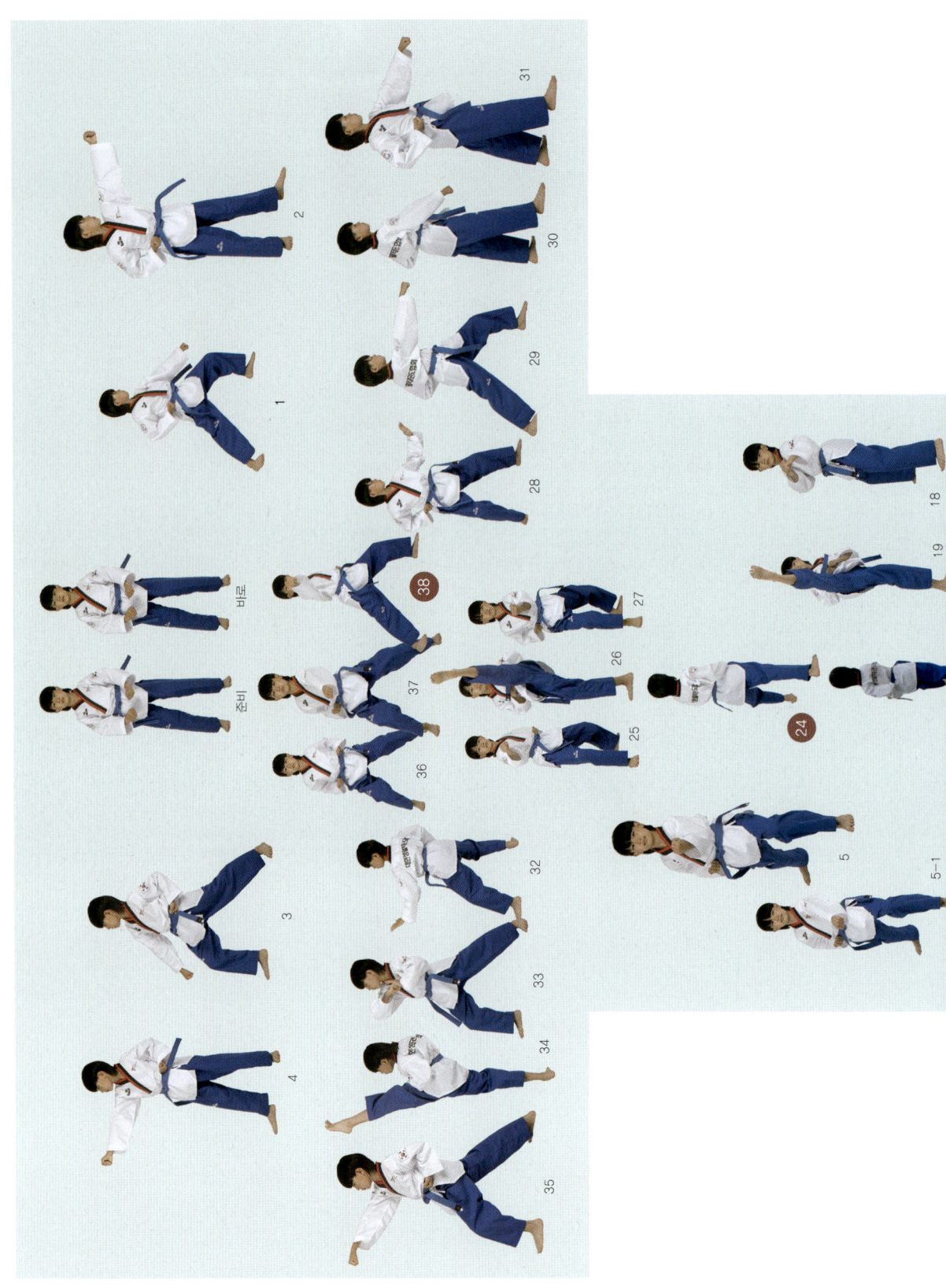

22 신품새

생태 품새 II : 파란 띠 과정

생태 품새 II 요약 설명

순서	시선	위치	서 기	동 작	품 명
준비	북	북	나란히 서기	한발 벌려	기본 준비 서기
1	서	서	왼 앞굽이	왼발 옮겨딛어	왼 내려막기
2	서	서	왼 서기	왼 한발 당겨	왼 메주먹 내려치기
3	동	동	오른 앞굽이	오른발 돌아 옮겨 딛어	오른 내려막기
4	동	동	오른 서기	오른 한발 당겨	오른 메주먹 내려치기
5-5⁻¹	북	북	왼 앞굽이	왼발 옮겨딛어왼 몸통 안막기	몸통 두번 지르기
6-6⁻¹	북	동북	오른 앞굽이	오른발 내딛어 오른 몸통 안막기	왼 몸통 안막기
7	동	북동	왼 앞굽이	왼발 뒤로 돌아 옮겨딛어	왼 올려막기
8-8⁻¹	동	동	오른앞굽이	오른발 금강 옆차기	왼 팔굽 표적치기
9	서	서	오른 앞굽이	오른발 뒤로 돌아 옮겨 딛어	왼 몸통 지르기
10	서	서	왼 앞굽이	왼발 내딛어	제비품 안치기
11-12	서	동	왼 앞서기	오른발 앞차고왼발 내딛어돌아서며	겨룸새
13	동	동	겨룸새	왼발 교차 딛고 오른발 내딛어	겨룸새[기합]
14	북	북	겨룸새	오른발 옮겨 딛고	겨룸새
15	북	북	겨룸새	양발 물러딛어 오른발 돌려차고 두 번 제자리 딛기	겨룸새
16-17-18	북	북	겨룸새	왼발 내딛었다 물러 딛고 오른발 물러딛어	겨룸새
19-20-21-22	북 북 남	북 북 남	겨룸새	오른발 앞차고 왼발 앞찬 다음 오른발 돌려차고 왼발 돌아딛어	손날 거들어 몸통 바깥막기
23	남	남	오른 앞굽이	오른발 내딛어	편손 끝 세워 찌르기
23⁻¹ 23⁻² 24	남	남	왼 앞굽이	왼발 내딛어 내려막고, 오른 몸통지르고	왼손 얼굴 지르기[기합]
25	북	북	왼 뒷굽이	오른발 뒤로 돌아딛어	오른 몸통 바깥막기
26-27	북	북	왼 뒷굽이	왼발 앞차고 제자리 내려놓으며	왼 몸통 안막기
28-29	서	서	오른 뒷굽이	왼 손날 몸통 바깥막고 왼발 내밀며	오른 몸통 지르기
30-31	서	서	오른 앞서기	오른발 내딛어 오른 내려막고	왼 몸통지르기

신품새

32	동	동	오른 뒷굽이	왼발 돌아 옮겨딛어	왼 손날 바깥막기
33	동	동	오른 앞굽이	오른발 내딛어	오른 팔굽 턱치기
34-35	동	동	왼 앞굽이	왼발 앞차고 내딛어	오른 얼굴 지르기
36	북	북	주춤서기	왼발 돌아 옮겨 딛어 양주먹 당기며	주춤서기
37	북	북	주춤서기	제자리	왼 몸통 지르기
38	북	서	왼 앞굽이	왼발 내밀며	오른 얼굴 지르기[기합]
바로	북	북	나란히 서기	왼발 당겨	기본 준비 서기

생태 품새 Ⅲ : 빨간 띠 과정

- 품새 선: ✚
- 권장 시간 : 56초
- 품새의 구성

6~8장의 비틀어막기, 외산틀막기, 당겨지르기, 젖혀지르기 등과 같은 핵심 기술에 물러딛기, 물러딛기, 돌아딛기 등과 앞차기, 뛰어 앞차기, 돌려차기, 내려차기를 다양하게 결합한 섞어차기를 보충하여 손기술과 발기술이 역동적이면서도 균형 있게 발휘되도록 구성하여 유급자 수준의 핵심 손발 기술을 종합적으로 익힐 수 있도록 구성하였다.

28　신품새

생태 품새 Ⅲ : 빨간 띠 과정

생태 품새 Ⅲ 요약 설명

순서	시선	위치	서 기	동작	품명
준비	북	북	나란히 서기	한발 벌려	기본 준비 서기
1	북	북	왼 앞굽이	옮겨딛어	오른 손날 비틀어 막기
2-3	북 남	남 남	왼 앞굽이	오른발 돌려차고 왼발 돌아 옮겨딛어	왼 내려막기
4	북	북	오른뒷굽이- 왼뒷굽이	오른발 내딛고- 왼발 돌아 옮겨딛어 거들어 몸통 바깥막고	오른 몸통 지르기
5-7	북	북	왼 앞굽이	두 발 당성차고(기합) 내딛어 왼 몸통 안막고	몸통 두번 지르기
8	북	북	왼 앞서기	왼발 당겨	왼 등주먹치기
9	북	북	주춤서기	오른발 표적차고 내딛어	오른팔굽 표적치기
10	북	북	오른 범서기	오른발 당겨 옮겨 딛어	왼 바탕손 안막기
11	서	서	왼 앞굽이	왼발 옮겨 딛어 왼 얼굴 바깥막고	오른 몸통 지르기
12-13	서	서	오른 앞굽이	오른발 앞차고 내딛어	왼 몸통 지르기
14	동	동	오른 앞굽이	오른발 뒤돌아 옮겨딛어	가위막기
15-16	동	동	왼 앞굽이	왼발 앞차고 내딛어	오른 몸통 지르기
17	북	북	오른 뒷굽이	왼발 옮겨딛어	왼 손날 바깥막기(4초)
18	북	북	왼 앞굽이	왼발 내밀며 오른 팔굽턱치고 오른 등주먹 앞치고	왼 몸통 지르기
19	북	북	겨룸새	왼발당기며 양주먹 뒤로빼서	겨룸새[기합]
20-21	북	북	겨룸새	제자리 딛고 두 번 발바꿔 딛고 양발 물러 딛고 뒤로 돌아 왼발 내 옮겨딛기	겨룸새
22-23-24	북	북	왼 뒷굽이	왼발 돌려찬 다음 오른발 내려차고 내딛어	거들어내려막기
25-26	북	북	모아서기	왼발 앞차고 오른발 뛰어 앞차고(기합) 왼발 당겨	보주먹(4초)
27	남	남	오른 뒷굽이	왼발 돌아 옮겨 딛어	손날 거들어 내려막기
28	남	남	왼 뒷굽이	오른발 내딛어	손날 거들어 내려막기
29	남	남	주춤서기	왼발 옮겨딛어	왼손날 옆막기
30	북	북	오른 범서기	오른발 옮겨딛어	손날 거들어 몸통 바깥막기

31-32-33	북	북	오른 앞굽이 오른 범서기	오른발 앞차고 왼 몸통지르고 오른발 당기며	오른 바탕손 안막기
34-35	북	남	왼 앞굽이 오른 앞굽이	왼발 물러딛어 외산틀막고	왼 몸통 지르기[기합]
바로	북	북	나란히 서기	왼발 당겨	기본 준비 서기

생태 품새 Ⅳ : 1단 과정

- 품새 선: 不
- 권장 시간 : 71초
- 품새의 구성

고려 품새의 손날바깥치기, 한손날아래막기, 무릎눌러꺾기, 칼재비, 거듭옆차기 등과 같은 핵심 기술에 손날목치가, 제비품안치기, 날개펴기, 헤쳐막기 등과 돌려차고 뒷주먹 지르기, 표적지르고 거듭 옆차기, 물러딛고 돌려차기, 물러딛고 나래차기, 내딛고 물러딛은 다음 돌려차기 등과 같은 연결 기술을 보충하여 빠르게 진행함으로써 고려 품새의 역동성을 체험하며 신속한 상황 대응 능력을 기를 수 있도록 구성하였다.

34 신품새

12 34 48 51 기합

생태 품새 Ⅳ : 1단 과정

생태 품새 IV 요약 설명

순서	시선	위치	서 기	동 작	품 명
준비	북	북	나란히 서기	한발 벌려	통밀기
1	서	서	왼 앞서기	왼발 내딛어	왼 손날 내려막기
2	서	서	오른 앞굽이	오른발 내딛어	오른손 칼재비
3	동	동	오른 앞서기	오른발 뒤로 돌아 옮겨딛어	오른 손날 내려막기
4	동	동	왼 앞굽이	왼발 내딛어	왼손 칼재비
5	북	북	왼 범서기	왼발 옮겨딛어	오른 관절꺾기
6-7	북	북	왼 범서기 오른앞굽이	오른 앞차고 내딛어	금강몸통지르기
8-8⁻¹	북	북	모아서기 주춤서기	왼발 당겨 양손 원 그리며 가슴에 교차시켜 오른발 물러딛고 왼발 물러딛어 주춤서며	아래 헤쳐막기
9	서북	서북	오른 뒷굽이	양 무릎 피며 왼발 옮겨딛어	손날 거들어 몸통 바깥막기
10	서북	서북	오른 앞굽이	오른발 내딛어	제비품 안치기
11-12	서북	서북	오른 앞굽이	오른 엎은 손날 바깥치고	왼 몸통 지르기(기합)
13	동남	동남	왼 앞굽이	옮겨딛어 왼손날 바깥치고	왼손날 내려막기
14	동남	동남	오른 앞굽이	오른발 내딛어 오른손날 목치고	오른 손날 내려막기
15	북	북	모아서기	왼발 옮겨딛어	날개펴기
16	북	북	오른 앞굽이	왼발 물러딛어	몸동 헤쳐막기
17-18	북	북	왼 앞굽이	왼발 돌려차고 내딛어	오른 얼굴 지르기
19	동북	동북	왼 뒷굽이	오른발 내딛어	손날 거들어 몸통 바깥 막기
20	동북	동북	왼 앞굽이	왼발 내딛어	제비품 안치기
21-22	동북	동북	왼 앞굽이	왼발 내딛어 왼 엎은 손날 바깥치고	오른 몸통 지르기
23	서남	서남	오른 앞굽이	오른발 옮겨 딛어 오른 엎은 손날 바깥치고	오른손날 내려막기
24-24⁻¹	서남	서남	왼 앞굽이	왼발 내딛어 왼손날 목치고	왼 손날 내려막기
25-26	남	남	주춤서기	오른발 옮겨 딛어 왼 손날옆막고	표적 지르기

27-28-29	남 북	남 서	앞 꼬아서기 주춤서기	오른발 앞 꼬아 서며 거듭 옆차고 내딛어 손날 옆막고	표적 지르기
30-32	북	북	앞 꼬아서기 오른 앞굽이 오른 앞서기	왼 앞꼬아 서며 거듭 옆차고 내딛어 편 손끝 젖혀 찌르고 오른발 당겨	오른 내려막기
33-34	북	북	왼 앞서기	왼발 내딛어 왼 바탕손 눌러막고 왼발 뒤로 물러딛어	겨룸새[기합]
35	북	북	겨룸새	앞발 내밀었다 당겨딛고 발바꿔 딛어	겨룸새
36-37	북	북	겨룸새 왼 앞굽이	양발 물러딛어 나래차고	왼주먹 내려막으며 오른주먹몸통지르기
38	북	북	겨룸새	두번 제자리 딛고 발바꿔 딛어	겨룸새
39-40	북	북	겨룸새	양발 물러딛어 오른발 돌려차고	오른주먹 내려막고 왼주먹 몸통지르기
41-42-43	북	북	모아서기	왼발 당기며 양손 엇걸어 막고 오른 손날 옆치고	왼 손날 위로 찌르기
44	남	남	오른 앞서기	뒤로 돌아 옮겨딛어 무릎앉아	내려지르기
45	남	남	오른 무릎 앉기	오른발 내딛어	날개펴기
46-47	북 동	북 동	왼 앞굽이 오른 앞굽이	뒤로돌아 왼발 옮겨딛고 왼 내려막고 오른발 옮겨딛어	왼팔굽표적치기
48	북	동북	왼 앞굽이 오른 앞굽이	왼손 내리고 오른 칼제비	왼 얼굴 지르기[기합]
49	북	북	모아서기	오른발 옮겨딛어	메주먹 표적치기(8초)
50	남	남	오른 앞서기	오른발 뒤로돌아 옮겨 딛어	아래 헤쳐막기
51	북	북	왼 앞굽이	왼발 뒤로돌아 옮겨딛어	오른 칼제비[기합]
바로	북	북	나란히 서기	오른발 당겨	통밀기

생태 품새 IV : 1단 과정

생태 품새 V : 2단 과정

- 품새 선: 兄
- 권장 시간 : 71초
- 품새의 구성

금강 품새는 학다리서기 금강막기, 주춤서기 산틀막기, 주춤서기 큰돌쩌귀, 안팔목 헤쳐 막기 등의 기술로 매우 단조롭게 구성되어 있다. 따라서 생태 품새 V는 금강 품새의 주요 기술에 바탕손 턱치기, 편손 산틀막기, 손날 엇걸어 산틀막기 등의 손기술을 더하고 내딛기, 물러딛기, 내딛고 물러딛기, 돌아딛기 등과 결합한 돌려차기, 앞발들어 앞차기, 돌개차기 등의 차기 기술을 보충하여 무겁게 진행함으로써 금강 품새의 강렬함과 태권도 공방 기술의 강인함을 체험할 수 있도록 구성하였다.

40   신품새

생태 품새 V : 2단 과정

생태 품새 V 요약 설명

순서	시선	위치	서 기	동 작	품 명
준비	북	북	나란히 서기	한발 벌려	기본 준비 서기
1	서	북	주춤 서기	왼발 옮겨 딛어	왼 금강 내려 막기
2	서	서	왼 앞굽이	왼발 옮겨 딛어	오른 몸통 지르기
3	서	서	오른 앞굽이	오른발 내딛어	오른 턱치기
4	북	북	주춤 서기	왼발 옮겨딛어	몸통 헤쳐 막기
5	동	북	주춤 서기	제자리	오른 금강 내려 막기
6	동	동	오른 앞굽이	오른발 옮겨 딛어	왼 몸통 지르기
7	동	동	왼 앞굽이	왼발 내딛어	왼 턱치기
8-9-10	동 북	동 북	나란히 서기	오른발 옆차고 주춤서 몸통 헤쳐막고 오른발 당겨	아래 헤쳐막기(4초)
11	서북	서북	겨룸새	오른발 옮겨딛어	겨룸새[기합]
12-13	서북	서북	겨룸새	끌어 돌려차고	오른발 돌려차기
14-15	서북	서북	겨룸새 오른 앞굽이	양발 물러딛고 발바꿔 오른발 뒤로 돌아 옮겨 딛어	오른팔 내려막으며 왼주먹 몸통지르기
16-17	서북 남	서북 남	나란히 서기	오른발 돌개차고 내딛어	아래 헤쳐막기
18	동	동	모아서기 왼 앞굽이	오른발 옮겨 딛어 가슴앞 양손 교차하고 왼발 내딛어	몸통 헤쳐막기
19	동	동	오른 앞굽이	오른발 내딛어 오른 바탕손 턱치고	왼 바탕손 턱치기
20	동	동	왼 앞굽이	왼발 내딛어	오른 몸통 지르기
21	동	북	주춤서기	오른발 옮겨돌아 딛어	큰 돌쩌귀
22-23	북	북	주춤 서기	왼손날 비틀어 바깥막고	손날엇걸어 내려막기
24-25	북	북	오른 범서기	오른발 옮겨 딛어 오른 외산틀막고	왼 외산틀막기
26	북	북	주춤서기	오른발 짓찧고	산틀막기[기합]
27	동북	동북	오른 앞굽이	왼발 교차딛고 오른발 내딛어	거들어 바탕손 턱치기
28	서남	서남	왼 앞굽이	왼발 돌아 옮겨딛어	아래 헤쳐막기

29	서북	서북	주춤서기	오른발 내딛고 왼발 내딛어	엇걸어 산틀막기
30-31	서남북	서남북	왼 앞서기 범서기 주춤서기	왼발 내딛어 바탕손 눌러막고 오른발 돌아 디디며 양손날 교차막고 왼발 옮겨딛어	양손날 산틀막기
32-33-34	동	북	주춤서기	멍에치고 왼 큰 돌쩌귀, 오른쪽으로 돌아딛어	왼 큰 돌쩌귀
35-36	서북 서북	서북 동	왼 앞굽이	왼발 내딛어 거들어 오른 얼굴 지르고	오른 메주먹 내려치기
37	북	동	주춤서기	왼발 옮겨딛어	산틀막기(기합)
38-39	북	북	왼 범서기 나란히 서기	왼발 당겨딛어 몸통 헤쳐막고 오른발 당겨	아래 헤쳐막기(4초)
40	서	북	오른 학다리서기	왼발 당겨 붙이며	금강 내려막기(8초)
41-42-43	서	북	주춤서기	왼발 앞차고 왼발 내려딛어 오른 큰 돌쩌귀, 왼 한발 돌아 디디며	오른 큰 돌쩌귀
44	북	북	오른 뒷굽이	오른발 뒤로 옮겨딛어	왼 손날 안막기
45-46-47	북	북	왼 뒷굽이	왼발 뒤로 물러딛어 오른 손날 안막고, 오른 손날 얼굴막고	왼 주먹 들어 올리기
48-49-50 -51-52 -53-54	동	북	학다리 서기 오른 앞굽이 오른-왼 앞서기 주춤서기	금강내려막고[4초] 오른발 들어 앞 차고 내딛어 얼굴 두 번 지르고 오른발 당기며 오른 몸통-왼 몸통 연속 지르고 왼발 옮겨딛어	왼 돌쩌귀[기합]
바로	북	북	나란히 서기	오른발 옮겨 딛어	기본 준비 서기

생태 품새 VI : 3단 과정

- 품새 선:
- 권장 시간 : 69초
- 품새의 구성

 테백 품새는 손날아래 헤쳐막기, 금강 몸통막기, 가위막기, 당겨 턱지르기, 제비품 목치기, 손날 엎어꺾기 등 두 손으로 막고, 지르고, 치는 동작 중심으로 다소 어렵지만 단조롭게 구성되어 있다. 따라서 생태 품새 VI에서는 태백 품새의 핵심 동작에 제비품안치기, 날개 펴기, 한손날 목치기, 손날아래 헤쳐막기 등을 추가하여 다양하게 재구성하고 돌려차기, 나래차기, 뒤차기 등을 제자리 딛기, 내딛기, 물러딛기, 내딛고 물리딛기 등과 결합하여 중속도로 온건하게 진행함으로써 태백 품새의 굳건함과 태권도 공방 기술의 비상함을 체험할 수 있도록 구성하였다.

46　신품새

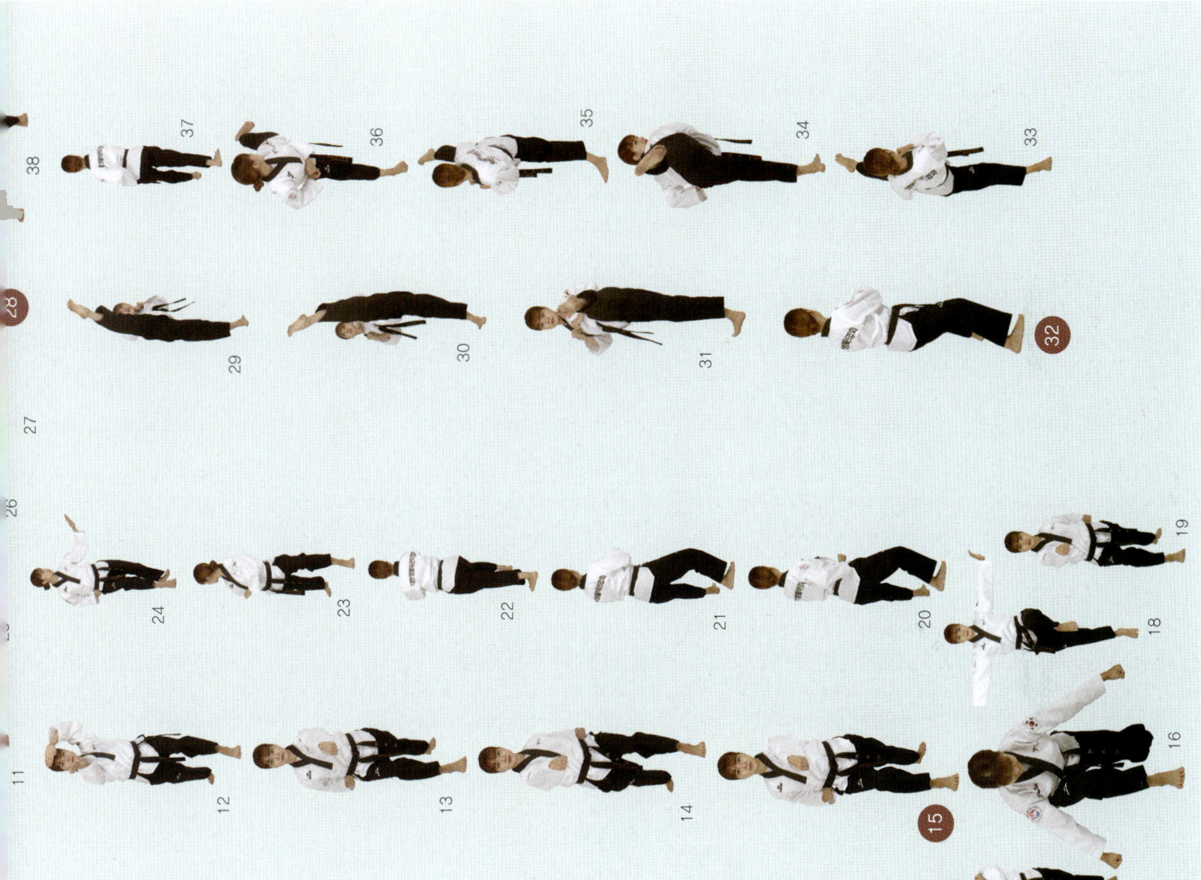
11
12
13
14
15
16
17
18
19
20
21
22
23
24
26
27
29
30
31
32
33
34
35
36
37
38

15 28 32 기합

생태 품새 VI 요약 설명

순서	시선	위치	서 기	동작	품명
준비	북	북	나란히 서기	한발 벌려	기본 준비 서기
1-2 -3-4	북 서북 북 동	동북 서북 서북 동	오른 앞굽이 왼 앞굽이 오른 앞굽이	오른발 옮겨딛어 왼 손날 옆치고 거들어 칼제비 오른 올려 막고 오른 무릎 구부려	왼 내려 지르기
5	서	서	왼 범서기	왼발 옮겨딛어	손날 아래 헤쳐막기
6-7	서	서	오른 앞굽이	오른발 앞차고 내딛어	몸통 두번 지르기
8	동	동	오른 범서기	오른발 뒤로 돌아 옮겨 딛어	가위 막기
9-10	동	동	왼 앞굽이	왼발 앞차고 내딛어	몸통 두번 지르기
11	북	북	오른 뒷굽이	왼발 옮겨딛어	금강 몸통 막기
12	북	북	왼 앞굽이	왼발 내밀며	제비품 안치기
13	북	북	오른 앞굽이	오른발 내딛어 오른 손목 제쳐 틀며	왼 몸통 지르기
14	북	북	왼 앞굽이	왼발 내딛어 왼 손목 제쳐 틀며	오른 몸통 지르기
15	북	북	오른 앞굽이	오른발 내딛어 오른 손목 제쳐 틀며	왼 몸통 지르기[기합]
16	북	북	오른 앞굽이	제자리 무릎 구부리며	양 주먹 아래 헤쳐막기
17-18	북	북	왼 학다리서기	왼 무릎 뛰며 교차 막고	날개 펴기
19	북	북	오른 앞굽이	왼발 물러 딛어	오른 몸통 지르기
20	남	남	오른 뒷굽이	왼발 돌아 옮겨딛어	왼 등주먹 치기
21	남	남	오른 뒷굽이	오른발 내딛고 왼발 내딛어	손날 거들어 몸통막기
22	남	남	오른 앞굽이	오른발 내딛어	편손끝 세워 찌르기
23	남	북	왼 앞굽이	왼발 뒤로 옮겨 딛고	잡힌 손목 밑으로 빼기
24	서	북	오른 범서기	왼발 당겨	왼 손날 막기(2초)
25	북	북	왼 뒷굽이	오른발 내밀며	왼 당겨 턱 지르기(4초)
26-27	북	북	왼 뒷굽이 오른 앞굽이	오른 몸통 지르기(2초) 오른발 내밀며	몸통 두번 지르기
28	남	남	겨룸새	왼발 내딛어 두 번 제자리 딛고	겨룸새[기합]

29-30 -31-32	북 남	북 남	겨룸새	오른발 돌려차고 왼발 돌려차고 양발 물러딛고 나래차고 오른발 내딛고 돌아 옮겨딛어	겨룸새[기합]
33-34 -35-36 -37-38	남 남 북	남 북 북	겨룸새 왼 앞굽이 주춤서기	두 번 제자리 딛고 왼발 끌어 돌려차고 오른발 뒤차고 양발 물러딛고 오른발 돌려차고 왼발 뒷차고 오른몸통 지르고 왼발 뒤로 돌아 옮겨딛어	아래 헤쳐막기
39	동	동	왼 뒷굽이	오른발 틀며	손날 거들어 몸통 바깥막기
40	동	동	오른 뒷굽이	왼발 내딛어	금강 몸통 막기
41-42 -43-44	동	동	오른 뒷굽이 오른 학다리서기 왼 앞굽이	당겨 턱 지르고 왼 몸통 지르고 왼발 당겨 오른 작은 돌쩌귀 왼발 금강 옆차고 내딛어	오른 팔굽 표적치기
45	서	서	오른 범서기	오른발 뒤로 돌아 당겨 딛어	왼 관절 꺾기
46-47	서	서	왼 앞굽이 뒤꼬아서기	왼발 내딛어 몸통 헤쳐막고 오른발 뒷 꼬아서고	제쳐 지르기
48	서	서	오른 뒷굽이	오른발 물러딛어	손날 거들어 몸통 바깥막기
49-50 -51-52 -53	서	서	왼 뒷굽이 왼 학다리서기 오른 앞굽이	오른발 내딛어 금강 몸통 막고 당겨 턱 지르고 오른 몸통 지르고 오른발 당겨 왼 작은 돌쩌귀 오른발 금강 옆차고 내딛어	왼팔굽 표적치기
54	북	북	오른 범서기	오른발 돌아 옮겨딛어	손날 아래 헤쳐 막기
바로	북	북	나란히 서기	왼발 당겨	기본 준비 서기

생태 품새 Ⅶ : 4단 과정

- 품새 선: 工
- 권장 시간 : 71초
- 품새의 구성

평원 품새는 팔굽 올려치기, 거들어 얼굴막기, 등주먹 당겨치기, 멍에치기, 헤쳐 산틀막기 등의 기술을 부드럽게 수련하도록 구성한 품새이다. 생태 품새 Ⅶ은 평원 품새의 주요 기술에 다양한 거들어막기, 손날막기, 엇걸러 막기 등과 같은 손기술과 내딛기, 물러딛기, 돌아딛기 등과 결합한 빠른 발 돌려차기, 뒤후려차기, 뒤차기 등과 같은 발차기 기술을 균형있게 배치하여 전반부에서는 기술을 역동적으로 발휘하고 후빈부에서는 기술을 부드럽고 온화하게 수행하는 가운데 평원 품새의 격정과 평온, 위협과 평화의 대립적 의미를 깊이 체험할 수 있도록 구성하였다.

52 신품새

④ ⑧ ⑬ ㊼ ㊾ 기합

생태 품새 Ⅶ : 4단 과정 53

생태 품새 VII 요약 설명

순서	시선	위치	서 기	동작	품 명
준비	북	북	나란히 서기	한발 벌려	기본 준비 서기
1	북	북	주춤 서기	양 주먹 당겨	주춤 서기
2-3-4	북	북	주춤 서기	몸통 두번 지르고 왼 얼굴 지르고 오른 작은 돌쩌귀	금강 지르기[기합]
5-6-7-8	북 북 북	동북 서북 서북	오른 앞굽이 주춤서기 오른 앞굽이	오른발 틀며 왼손날 내려막고 오른몸통 지르고 왼팔굽 올려치고 왼 앞굽이	오른 얼굴지르기[기합]
9-10-11-12	동 서 북 북	북 북 북 북	왼 뒤꼬아 서기 오른 앞서기	왼발뒤로 옮겨딛어 손날 거들어 몸통 바깥막고 오른 손날 거들어 내려막기 오른 손날 얼굴막고 왼발 물러딛어	오른 손날 내려막기(3초)
13	북	북	겨룸새	왼발 물러 딛어	겨룸새(기합)
14	북	북	겨룸새	제자리 두번 딛고 발바꿔 딛기	겨룸새
15-16-17-18	북	북	겨룸새	끌어 돌려차고 오른발 돌려차고 왼발 뒤후려차고 오른발 내딛고 왼발 내딛어 왼 곁다리 서며	날개 펴기
19-20-21-22	북 동 서	서북 동 서	왼 앞굽이 오른 앞 서기	왼발 옮겨딛어 오른손날 내려막고 오른발 끌어 왼손 끝 내리 찌르고 오른발 물러딛어 왼발 뒷차고	왼팔 내려막으며 오른주먹 몸통지르기
23-24	서 서	서북 서북	나란히 서기	왼발 돌아 딛고 오른발 뒤 후려차고	왼 내려 막기(4초)
25-26-27	동북 북 북	동북 북 북	오른 앞굽이 왼 뒷꼬아서기 주춤서기	오른발 내딛어 왼 관절 꺾고 왼발 옮겨딛어 왼 등주먹 치고 오른발 옮겨딛	가위 막기
28-29-30	동	동	오른 앞서기 왼 범서기	오른발 옮겨 딛어 오른 등주먹 치고 왼발 표적 차고, 오른발-왼발 내딛어	왼 바탕손 안 막기
31	북	북	주춤서기	오른발 내딛어	엇걸어 산틀막기
32	동	북	왼 앞꼬아서기	왼발 옮겨딛어	멍에치기
33-34-35-36-37	북서 북 서	북 북북 북 서	왼 앞 꼬아서기 주춤서기 왼 범서기	엇걸어 올려막고 오른발 옮겨딛어 엇걸어 내려막고 오른 손날 옆치고 왼 얼굴막고 왼발 돌아 당겨딛어	오른 몸통 지르기
38	서	서	왼 앞굽이	왼발 내밀며	오른 팔굽 올려치기
39-40-41	서	서	겨룸새	오른발 앞차고왼발 금강 옆차고 내딛어	오른 팔굽 표적 치기

42	북	북	왼 뒷굽이	오른발 당겨 왼발 물러딛어	손날 거들어 몸통 바깥막기
43	북	북	오른 뒷굽이	오른발 물러딛어	손날 거들어 내려막기
44-45	북	북	오른 앞굽이	왼발 물러딛어 오른 팔굽 올려치고	왼 팔굽 턱치기
46	북	북	주춤서기	오른발 당겨딛어	거들어 옆막기[2초]
47-47⁻¹	북	북	주춤서기	오른발 짓찧고 오른 등주먹 거들어 앞치고[기합]	왼 등주먹 거들어 앞치기
48-49	동	북	왼 앞꼬아서기 주춤서기	왼발 옮겨딛어 멍에치고 오른발 옮겨딛어	엇걸어 산틀막기
50	동	동	오른 앞굽이	오른발 옮겨딛어	왼 팔굽 올려치기
51-52-53	동 서	동 서	오른 뒷굽이 오른 뒷굽이	왼발 앞차고 뒤돌아 오른발 옆차고 손날 거들어 몸통 바깥막고	손날 거들어 내려막기[4초]
54	서	서	왼 앞굽이	왼발 내밀며	오른 몸통 지르기
55-56	서	서	오른 앞굽이	오른발 옆차고 내딛어	왼 팔굽 올려치기
57-58	서 서	서 북	오른 앞굽이 주춤서기	왼발 내딛어 오른 바탕손 턱치고 오른발 내딛고 왼발 옮겨딛어	거들어 옆막기[2초]
59-59⁻¹	북	북	주춤서기	왼발 짓찧고 왼 등주먹 거들어 앞치고[기합]	오른 등주먹 거들어 앞치기
60-61	서	북	오른 학다리서기	오른발 당겨붙혀 금강 내려막고	오른 작은 돌쩌귀
62-63	서	서	오른 학다리서기 왼 앞굽이	왼 등주먹 치고 왼발 옮겨딛어	오른 얼굴 지르기
64-65	서 서 동	서 서 동	오른 뒷굽이	오른발 앞차고 왼발 뒤돌아 옆차고 손날 거들어 몸통 바깥막고	오른 손날 거들어 내려막기
66	동	남	주춤서기	왼발 옮겨딛어	엇걸어 산틀 막기
67-68	동	남	오른 앞꼬아서기 오른 앞서기	오른발 옮겨 딛어 멍에치고 왼발 돌아 옮겨딛고 오른발 내딛어	오른 내려 막기[2초]
바로	북	북	나란히 서기	왼발 당겨	기본 준비 서기

● 개발진 소개 •••

손 천 택

약력

오하이오주립대학교 박사
인천대학교 체육교육과 교수
국기원 태권도연구소 소장
국기원 이사 · 원장직무대행
한국스포츠교육학회 회장
대한생활태권도협회 회장
대학태권도연맹 전무이사
인천 아시안게임 경기사무차장

지 현 철

한국체육대학교 사회체육대학원 태권도학과 석사
국기원 고단자 심사분과 부위원장
서울시태권도협회 품새분과 수석 부의장
세계태권도연맹 품새 국제심판
대한생활태권도협회 부회장
새암 체육관장
강동구태권도협회장
글로벌신문사 부회장

지 수 민

가천대학교 운동치료학 석사
서울시 생활 태권도 협회 시범단
강동구 태권도 시범단 코치
아디다스 태권체조 주 강사
아르태 태권무 공연팀 주장
대한생활태권도협회 시범 분과 위원장

KTAA Taekwondo **Modern Poomsae**

First edition September 15, 2022

Developer Hyunchul Ji · Soomin Ji
Supervisor Cheontaik Son
Publisher Sangphil Moon
Design editor Inmoon Sohn

Publishing Company Sang-A Corporation
Registration Number No. 318-1997-000041Ho
Address #715 Center plus, 3-4, Gyeongin-ro 82-gil,
    Yeongdeungpo-gu, Seoul, 07371 Korea.
E-mail 0221642700@daum.net
www.tkdsanga.com

ISBN 979-11-86196-23-6 13690
Price 20,000won ($20)

Printed in Korea

KTAA Taekwondo
Modern Poomsae

Developer   Hyunchul Ji · Soomin Ji
Supervisor Cheontaik Son

Korea Taekwondo for All Association

CONTENTS

I. Overview of Modern Poomsae 6

1. Meaning of Modern Poomsae 6
2. Necessity of Developing Modern Poomsae 6
3. Expected Effects of Modern Poomsae 7
4. Principles of Developing Modern Poomsae 8

II. Modern Poomsae 11

KTAA Poomsae I : Yellow Belt Poomsae 12
KTAA Poomsae II : Blue Belt Poomsae 18
KTAA Poomsae III : Red Belt Poomsae 24
KTAA Poomsae IV : 1st Black Belt Poomsae 30
KTAA Poomsae V : 2nd Black Belt Poomsae 36
KTAA Poomsae VI : 3rd Black Belt Poomsae 42
KTAA Poomsae VII : 4th Black Belt Poomsae 48

I. Overview of Modern Poomsae

II. Modern Poomsae

I. Overview of Modern Poomsae

1. Meaning of Modern Poomsae

'Modern Poomsae' is a concept that contrasts with traditional Poomsae, meaning that it is a newly developed Poomsae reflecting the reality of Taekwondo techniques. While the Poomsae developed in preparation for the 2018 Asian Games is a 'New Poomsae' with a completely different intention and purpose from the existing Poomsae, the 'Modern Poomsae' respects the purpose and content system of the existing Poomsae and acknowledges its legitimacy. In the meantime, it refers to the Pomsae that can be easily learned by ordinary students at the Taekwondo school. In other words, 'Modern Poomsae' is a creative Poomsae developed by combining the core techniques of certified Poomsae of Kukkiwon with new techniques developed over the years. The 'Modern Poomsae' is developed with an emphasis on motivating students to practice Poomsae and encouraging them to practice certified Poomsae of Kukkiwon more actively.

2. Necessity of Developing Modern Poomsae

Poomsae is a learning frame for practicing the Taekwondo techniques needed to protect oneself or attack an opponent by being against a virtual enemy. However, with the development of culture and Taekwondo techniques, the intention or purpose of Poomsae learning has changed significantly. An increasing number of students learn Poomsae for various purposes, such as pursuing character education values or expressing aesthetic values beyond simply developing self-defense techniques or gaining confidence.

Furthermore, as Taekwondo has been re-established as a martial art sport and developed into a core sport of the Olympics, various foot techniques have been developed through the process of competition. In addition, Poomsae has been adopted as an official event of the Asian Games through the process of holding regional Poomsae competitions as part of revitalizing the Taekwondo school. Now, Kukkiwon's certified Poomsae is not enough to be able to satisfy the students' desire to learn Poomsae.

Furthermore, with daily sports, the number of students who are trying to improve their health and their quality of life by happily learning Taekwondo has been increasing. However, the somewhat tedious and biased hand technique-centered Poomsae of Kukkiwon did not satisfy the various needs and expectations of students, so the request for the development of new Poomsae is increasing. In addition, the technical composition of the existing Poomsae, which is biased towards hand techniques, deepens and solidifies the division between Dojang-oriented daily Taekwondo and school athletes-oriented elite Taekwondo.

Therefore, the Korean Taekwondo for All Association(KTAA) has established a 'Modern Poomsae' that reflects new techniques developed through sparring competition, Poomsae competition, and demonstrating performances. In addition, it has tried to promote the desire for certified Poomsae learning and to more effectively achieve goals: the personality education goals, health education goals, and cultural and artistic goals that modern Taekwondo pursues.

3. Expected Effects of Modern Poomsae

Improving approach tendency. If the Taekwondo teachers make good use of 'Modern Poomsae', students can more easily access Taekwondo and Taekwondo Poomsae, and enjoy Poomsae learning. This is because 'Modern Poomsae' faithfully reflects the expectations of students by actively accepting and organizing various Taekwondo techniques developed so far.

Stimulating the desire for Poomsae learning. 'Modern Poomsae' is designed so that students can practice various hand and foot techniques to the music with joy, away from the boring and training-centered Poomsae learning caused by the monotonous composition of Kukkiwon Poomsae. Therefore, it has the advantage of stimulating the students' desire to practice Poomsae and allowing them to learn the skills they need to learn at each level in a fun way.

Acting as a stepping stone. 'Modern Poomsae' is reconstructed to music by adding new techniques to the core techniques of the existing Poomsae. Therefore, it has the effect of learning the core skills of the certified Kukkiwon Poomsae through the process of happily learning the 'Modern Poomsae'. This has the effect of encouraging students who avoid learning traditional Poomsae to practice the certified Poomsae of Kukkiwon more diligently by using the 'Modern Poomsae' as a stepping stone.

Implementing harmonious Taekwondo learning. 'Modern Poomsae' enables harmonious Taekwondo learning by integrating two domains of Taekwondo, which has been dualized with Taekwondo centered on Poomsae and Taekwondo centered on sparring, and Taekwondo centered on hand techniques and Taekwondo centered on kicks. This integrated approach has the effect of producing elite athletes even in the Taekwondo school.

Improve artistic expression. 'Modern Poomsae' helps students to master the basic skills necessary for Taekwondo performances, which are highly requested by the 21st century's cultural and welfare society. In other words, the Modern Poomsae can bring the effect of nurturing the artistic expression necessary for creative artistic activities beyond the dimensions of Taekwondo training effects such as increasing self-defense ability, improving health, and cultivating character.

4. Principles of Developing Modern Poomsae

'Modern Poomsae' is developed by setting the following principles of Poomsae development and establishing detailed guidelines to complement the defects of certified Poomsae of Kukkiwon and to enhance the effect of Poomsae learning.

Developing Poomsae that reflects the intentions of certified Poomsae.
'Modern Poomsae' is developed in a way that gradually increases the difficulty level in consideration of the intention of the Kukkiwon Poomsae and the developmental stage of the Taekwondo skill. The Poomsae I, II, and III of the Korea Taekwondo for All Association are developed by following the principle of yin and yang and taking advantage of the meaning of the eight trigrams. In addition, the KTAA Poomsae IV, V, VI, and VII are developed in accordance with the intentions of Goryeo, Geumgang, Taebaek, and Pyeongwon Poomsae to suit the intention of life-long Poomsae learning.

Developing Poomsae in conjunction with certified Poomsae of Kukkiwon.
'Modern Poomsae' develops Poomsae that assumes the attack and defense techniques are actual fighting, but also reflects the characteristics of sports. This is because Taekwondo, as a martial art, should not only be able to develop fighting ability to effectively hit the vital points and subdue the opponent, but also faithfully reflect the characteristics of Taekwondo competition. Therefore, various techniques newly developed through sparring competitions and Poomsae competitions are faithfully arranged on the Poomsae line, but does not deviate from the intention of traditional Poomsae.

Developing Poomsae that embodies various values of Taekwondo.
'Modern Poomsae' not only develops self-defense skills by learning attack and defense techniques on the premise of actual fighting, but also develops Poomsae that realizes values such as health promotion, personality education, and appreciation of Taekwondo performances pursued by Taekwondo school. In particular, it is developed so that students can practice Taekwondo as a daily sport or cultivate the potential of life-long Taekwondo as an adult. In other words, just as the traditional 'Hanbok' is made into a comfortable living Hanbok, the shortcomings of the traditional Poomsae of Kukkiwon have been supplemented and modernized to develop into a 'Modern Taekwondo Poomsae'.

Detailed Guidelines for Developing Modern Poomsae

① Develop Taekwondo Poomsae that recognizes and respects traditional Taekwondo techniques.

② Develop Taekwondo Poomsae that reflects important skills that are not reflected in the traditional Poomsae of Kukkiwon.

③ Develop Poomsae that actively reflects various new techniques developed through Sparring competition, Poomsae contest, Taekwondo demonstration or performance, etc.

④ Develop Poomsae that actively reflects skills and movements that are effective in self-defense and valuable even in life-long sport.

⑤ Develop Poomsae so that techniques and movements are arranged on the Poomsae line according to the principle of left-right symmetry for the balanced development of the body.

⑥ Develop Poomsae so that hand and foot skills are reflected in a balanced way and stepping skills are properly included.

⑦ Develop Poomsae that arranges the necessary movements on the Poomsae line which is not deviated from the 8 directions in a symmetrical structure. This is because Poomsae follows the yin and yang ideas, and the ideas are differentiated and appear as the Eight Trigrams for divination, and the Eight Trigrams have a thorough symmetrical structure.

II. Modern Poomsae

Level of Poomsae	Name of Poomsae	Poomsae line	Number of actions	Intention to develop Poomsae
KTAA Poomsae I	Yellow Belt Poomsae		35	The purpose of the modern yellow belt Poomsae is to realize the importance of the basics and the meaning of strong and soft while learning the basic techniques of block, punch, step, and kick.
KTAA Poomsae II	Blue Belt Poomsae		44	The purpose of the modern blue belt Poomsae is to realize the importance of the enthusiasm, majestic expression of power, and the quiet majesty while learning how to quickly and forcefully control various complex movements and connected movements.
KTAA Poomsae III	Red Belt Poomsae		37	The purpose of the modern red belt Poomsae is to realize the importance of the flexibility, magnificence, and growth while learning how to use the various hand and foot techniques to harmonize with stepping.
KTAA Poomsae IV	1st Black Belt Poomsae		35	The purpose of the modern Koryo Poomsae is to realize the spirit of Koryo Dynasty and the spirit of the Koryo people, awakening the scholarly spirit of justification-fidelity-royalty while learning how to use the special parts of the hands and feet to demonstrate unique attack and defense techniques in various ways.
KTAA Poomsae V	2nd Black Belt Poomsae		57	The purpose of the modern Keumgang Poomsae is to feel the spirit of Mt. Keumgang and realize the wisdom and virtues of a Taekwondoist while learning how to balance and control the speed of various hand and foot techniques composed of symmetrical or asymmetrical movements.
KTAA Poomsae VI	3rd Black Belt Poomsae		58	The purpose of the modern Taebaek Poomsae is to feel the spirit of Mt. Baekdu and strengthen the determination to practice the high ideal of Dangun, humanitarianism, while learning how to moderately perform complex movements at moderate speed.
KTAA Poomsae VII	4th Black Belt Poomsae		75	The purpose of the modern Pyongwon Poomsae is to realize the spirit of peace, which is softness overcomes intensity and serenity overcomes conflict while learning how to flexibly use intricately connected movements that contradict each other.

KTAA Poomsae I : Yellow Belt Poomsae

- Poomsae line: ⊥
- Recommended time : 50 Seconds
- Composition of Poomsae

The modern yellow belt Poomsae is designed to expand the learning range of beginning Taekwondo skills and further improve sparring skills by combining the core skills of Taegeuk 1 Jang and 2 Jang such as Ap-seogi(Walking stance), Naeryeo-makgi(Downward block), Momtong-makgi(Body block), Ollyeo-makgi (Upward block), Momtong-Jireugi(Middle punch), Ap-chagi(Front kick) and newly introduced skills such as Juchum-seogi & Momtong-Jieugi(Riding stance & Middle punch), Juchum-seogi & Ollyeo-makgi(Riding stance & High punch), Nae-ditgi(Forward step), and Dora-ditgi(Turning step), etc.

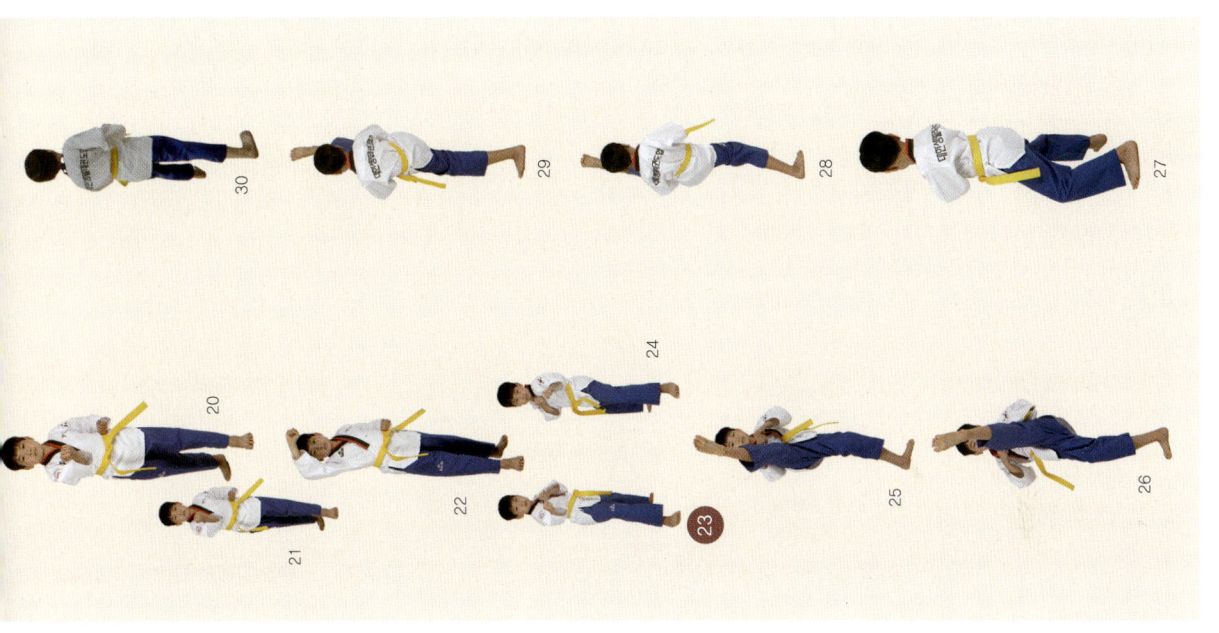

shout of concentration

KTAA Poomsae I : Yellow Belt Poomsae

KTAA Poomsae I : Yellow Belt Poomsae

Order	Eye direction	Body direction	Stance	Action	Name of pose
Ready	N	N	Parallel stance	One foot apart	Basic ready stance
1	N	N	Riding stance	Two fists pulled on the waist	Riding stance with two fists on the waist
2	N	N	Riding stance	While standing there	Left middle punch
3	N	N	Riding stance	While standing there	Right middle punch
4	N	N	Riding stance	While standing there	Middle middle high punch
5	N	N	Riding stance	While standing there	Middle middle high punch
6	N	N	Riding stance	While standing there	Left high punch
7	N	N	Parallel stance	Pull one foot	Parallel stance with two fists on the waist
8	W	W	Left walking stance	Move left foot	Right inward middle block
9	W	W	Right walking stance	Move right foot one step forward	Left middle punch
10	E	E	Right walking stance	Right foot move around the other side	Left middle block
11	E	E	Left walking stance	Left foot one step forward	Right middle punch
12	N	N	Left forward stance	Move left foot & downward block	Right middle punch
13	N	N	Right forward stance	Right foot one step forward	Middle punch [shout of concentration]
14	W	W	Left walking stance	Move left foot	Left downward block
15-16	W	W	Right forward stance	Right front kick & one step forward	Right hight punch
17	E	E	Right walking stance	Right foot move around the other side	Right downward block
18-19	E	E	Left forward stance	Left front kick & one step forward	Left high punch
20	N	N	Left walking stance	Move left foot	Right body block
21	N	N	Left walking stance	While standing there	Right body block (4 seconds)
22	N	N	Right walking stance	Right foot one step forward	Right upward block (4 seconds)

Modern Poomsae

23	N	N	Sparring stance	Left backward step	Sparring stance [shout of concentration]
24	N	N	Sparring stance	Switch step & step in place twice	Sparring stance
25-26	N	N	Sparring stance	Right front kick	Left font kick
27	S	S	Sparring stance	Turn around	Sparring stance
28-29	S	S	Sparring stance	Left front kick	Right front kick
30-31	S	S	Left forward stance	Left foot one step forward & downward block	Right middle punch
32	S	S	Right forwars stance	Right foot one step forward	Right middle punch [shout of concentration]
Stop	N	N	Parallel stance	Turn around with left foot	Basic ready stance

KTAA Poomsae II : Blue Belt Poomsae

- Poomsae line: ⊥
- Recommended time : 55 Seconds
- Composition of Poomsae

The modern blue belt Poomsae is designed to deepen and develop beginning skills of Taekwondo, promote sparring ability, and improve conscious understanding of skills with isometric exercises by combining simple blocking skills of Taegeuk 3-4 Jang and striking skills of the Taegeuk 4-5 Jang with various blocking skills and linking kicks such as Nae-ditgi & Ap-chagi(Forward step &Front kick), Nae-ditgi & Dollyeo-chagi(Forward step & Roundhouse kick), and Mulleo-ditgi & Naeryeo-chagi(Backward step & Downward kick), etc.

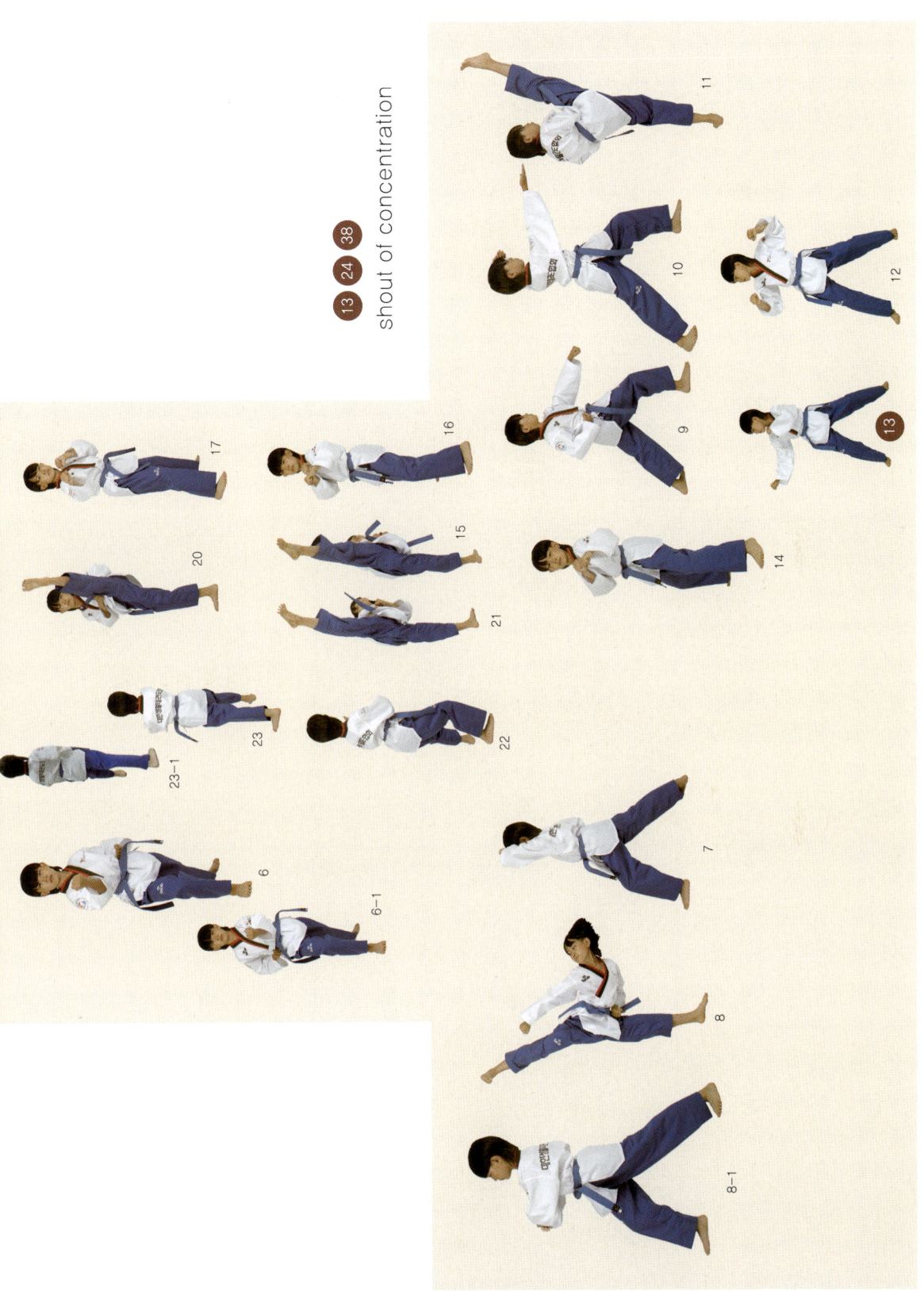

KTAA Poomsae II : Blue Belt Poomsae

KTAA Poomsae II : Blue Belt Poomsae

Order	Eye direction	Body direction	Stance	Action	Name of pose
Ready	N	N	Parallel stance	One foot apart	Basic ready stance
1	W	W	Left walking stance	Move left foot	Left downward block
2	W	W	Left stance	Pull in one foot	Strike down left hammer fist
3	E	E	Right forward stance	Move right foot around the other side	Right downward block
4	E	E	Right stance	Pull in one foot	Strike down with right hammer fist
5-5-1	N	N	Left forward stance	Move left foot & left inner body block	Double middle punch
6-6-1	N	N	Right forward stance	Right foot a step forward & inner body block	Left inner body block
7	E	E	Left forward stance	Turn around	Left high block
8-8-1	E	E	Right forward stance	Right diamond side kick	Left elbow target strike
9	W	W	Right forward stance	Right foot moves around	Left middle punch
10	W	W	Left forward stance	Left foot a step forward	Swallow pose neck strike
11-12	W	E	Left walking stance	Right front kick & left foot a step forward & turn around	Sparring stance
13	E	E	Sparring stance	Left foot cross over right foot & right foot a step forward	Sparring stance [shout of concentration]
14	N	N	Sparring stance	Move right foot around	Sparring stance
15	N	N	Sparring stance	A step backward & right roundhouse kick & step in pace twice	Sparring stance
16-17-18	N	N	Sparring stance	Left foot a step forward & a step backward, & right foot a step backward	Sparring stance
19-20-21-22	N S	N S	Sparring stance	Right front kick & left front kick & right roundhouse kick, turn around with left foot	'Hand knife' outer body block
23	S	S	Right forward stance	Right foot a step forward	Flat spear finger thrust
23-1 23-2 -24	S	S	Left forward stance	Left foot a step forward & downward block & right middle punch	Left high block [shout of concentration]
25	N	N	Left backward stance	turn around with right foot	Right outer block

26-27	N	N	Left backward stance	Left front kick & put it down	Left inner block
28-29	W	W	Right backward stance	Move left foot around & outer block with left 'hand knife', left foot slide out	Right middle punch
30-31	W	W	Right walking stance	Right foot a step forward & right downward block	Left middle punch
32	E	E	Right backward stance	Turn around & move left foot	Left 'hand knife' outer block
33	E	E	Right forward stance	Right foot a step forward	turning strike with right elbow
34-35	E	E	Left forward stance	Left front kick & a step forward	Right high punch
36	N	N	Riding stance	Move left foot around & pull two fists on the waist	Riding stance
37	N	N	Riding stance	While standing there	Left middle punch
38	N	W	Left forward stance	Slide out left foot slightly	Right high punch [shout of concentration]
Stop	N	N	Parallel stance	Pull left foot	Basic ready stance

KTAA Poomsae III : Red Belt Poomsae

- Poomsae line:

- Recommended time : 56 Seconds

- Composition of Poomsae

The modern red belt Poomsae is designed to ensure that hand and foot skills are demonstrated dynamically and harmoniously, so that color belt students can check core skills of the color belts and learn them comprehensively by supplementing key skills of the Taegeuk 6-8 Jang such as Biteureo-makgi (Twisting block), Hecheo-makgi(Double outward block), Oesanteul-makgi(Single mountain block), Geodeureo-makgi(Assisting block), Bakkat-makgi(Outward block), and Makgi & Jireugi (Blocking & punching) with mixed skills that combine Ap-chagi(Front kick) & (Roundhouse kick) with Nae-ditgi(Forward step), Dora-ditgi(Turing step), Mulleo-ditgi(Backward step), and Jejari-ditgi(Step in place).

shout of concentration

KTAA Poomsae III : Red Belt Poomsae

KTAA Poomsae III : Red Belt Poomsae

Order	Eye direction	Body direction	Stance	Action	Name of pose
Ready	N	N	Parallel stance	One foot apart	Basic ready stance
1	N	N	Left forward stance	Move left foot slightly	Right 'hand knife' twisting block
2-3	N	S	Left forward stance	Right roundhouse kick, move left foot around	Left downward block
4	N	N	Right back stance Left back stance	Right foot a step forward & left foot moves around, assisting outer block & left foot slides out slightly forward	Right middle punch
5-6-7	N	N	Left forward stance	Two feet alternated kick [shout of concentration] & left inner block	Middle punch twice
8	N	N	Left walking stance	Pull left foot	Left back fist strike
9	N	N	Riding stance	Right target kick & a step forward	Right elbow target strike
10	N	N	Right tiger stance	Pull right foot	Left palm hand inner block
11	W	W	Left forward stance	Move left foot & face outer block with left arm	Right middle punch
12-13	W	W	Right forward stance	Right front kick & a step forward	Left middle punch
14	E	E	Right forward stance	Turn right foot around the other side	Scissors block
15-16	E	E	Left forward stance	Left front kick	Right middle punch
17	N	N	Right back stance	Move left foot around	Left 'hand knife' outer block(4sec)
18	N	N	Left back stance	Right elbow chin strike with left foot sliding out & right back fist front strike	Left middle punch
19	N	N	Sparring stance	Two fists pull back	Sparring stance [shout of concentration]
20-21	N	N	Sparring stance	Step in place twice, switch step & backward step, turn around & move left foot a step forward	Sparring stance
22-23-24	N	N	Left back stance	Left roundhouse kick & right downward kick	Assisting downward block
25-26	N	N	Close stance	Left front kick & right jump front kick [shout of concentration], pull left foot	Covering fist (4sec)
27	S	S	Right back stance	Turn left foot around	Two 'hand knife' downward block

Modern Poomsae

28	S	S	Left back stance	Move right foot a step forward	Two 'hand knife' downward block
29	S	S	Riding stance	Move left foot slightly	Left 'hand knife' side block
30	N	N	Right tiger stance	Turn right foot around & a step backward	Two 'hand knife' outer block
31-32-33	N	N	Right forward stance right tiger stance	Right front kick & middle punch, pull right foot	Right palm hand inner block
34-35	N	S	Left forward stance right forward stance	Move left foot a step backward & single mountain block	Left middle punch [shout of concentration]
Stop	N	N	Parallel stance	Pull in left foot	Basic ready stance

KTAA Poomsae IV : 1ˢᵗ Black Belt Poomsae

- Poomsae line:
- Recommended time : 71 Seconds
- Composition of Poomsae

The modern Koryo Poomsae is designed to experience the dynamism of Goryo Poomsae and develop the ability to respond quickly to various situations by supplementing connected skills such as Dollyeo-chagi & Jireugi(Roundhouse kick and punch), Pyojeok-Jireugi & Narae-chagi(Double kick & punch), Mulleo-ditgi & Dollyeo-chagi & Jireugi(Backward step & roundhouse kick & punch), and Mulleo-ditgi & Narae-chagi & Jireugi(Backward step & double kick & punch) that combine the key techniques of Koryo poomsae such as Jebipum-chigi(Swallow poom neck strike), Jeocheo-Jireugi(Turn-over punch), and Sonnal Geodeureo- makgi (Assisting block with hand knife) with Jireugi(Punch) and Chagi(Kick).

12 34 48 51
shout of concentration

KTAA Poomsae IV : 1st Black Belt Poomsae

Order	Eye direction	Body direction	Stance	Action	Name of pose
Ready	N	N	Parallel stance	One foot apart	Log pushing posture
1	W	W	Left walking stance	Move left foot a step forward	Left 'hand knife' down block
2	W	W	Right forward stance	Move right foot a step forward	Right arc hand
3	E	E	Right walking stance	Move right foot around	Right 'hand knife' downward block
4	E	E	Left forward stance	Move left foot a step forward	Left arc hand
5	N	N	Left tiger stance	Move left foot around	Right joint snapping
6-7	N	N	Left tiger stance / Right forward stance	Right front kick & a step forward	Diamond middle punch
8-8-1	N	N	Close stance / Riding stance	Pull left foot & make a large circle with both hands and cross them in front of chest, move right foot a step backward & left foot a step backward. riding stance	Downward pushing block
9	NW	NW	Right back stance	Straighten two knees & move left foot around	Two 'hand knife' outer block
10	NW	NW	Right forward stance	Move right foot a step forward	Swallow pose inner strike
11-12	NW	NW	Right forward stance	Right upside-down 'hand knife' outward strike	Left middle punch [shout of concentration]
13	NE	SE	Left forward stance	Move left foot & left 'hand knife' outer strike	Left 'hand knife' downward block
14	NE	SE	Right forward stance	Move right foot a step forward & right 'hand knife' neck strike	Right 'hand knife' downward block
15	N	N	Close stance	Move left foot around	Wing spread
16	N	N	Right forward stance	Move left foot a step backward	Middle pushing block
17-18	N	N	Left forward stance	Left roundhouse kick & a step forward	Right high punch
19	NE	NE	Left back stance	Move right foot a step forward	Two 'hand knife' outer block
20	NE	NE	Left forward stance	Move left foot a step forward	Swallow pose inner strike
21-22	NE	NE	Left forward stance	Move left foot a step forward & left upside-down 'hand knife' outer strike	Right middle punch

23	SW	SW	Right forward stance	Move right foot & right upside-down 'hand knife' outer strike	Right 'hand knife' downward block
24-24¹	SW	SW	Left forward stance	Move left foot a step forward & left 'hand knife' neck strike	Left 'hand knife' downward block
25-26	S	S	Riding stance	Move right foot & left 'hand knife' side block	Target punch
27-28-29	S N	S W	Cross stance Riding stance	Cross stance with right foot front, double side kick & 'hand knife' side block	Target punch
30-32	N	N	Cross stance Right forward stance Right walking stance	Cross stance left foot front, double side kick & fingertip upward thrust, pull in right foot	Right downward block
33-34	N	N	Left walking stance	Move left foot a step forward & left palm hand pressing block, move left foot a step backward	Sparring stance [shout of concentration]
35	N	N	Sparring stance	Front foot slides out put it back & switch step	Sparring stance
36-37	N	N	Sparring stance Left forward stance	Move a step backward & double kick	Left arm downward block & right fist middle punch at a time
38	N	N	Sparring stance	Step in place twice & switch step	Sparring stance
39-40	N	N	Sparring stance	Move a step backward & right roundhouse kick	Right arm downward block & left fist middle punch at a time left 'hand knife' upward thrust
41-42-43	N	N	Close stance	Pull in left foot & two wrists crossed block, right 'hand knife' side strike	left 'hand knife' upward thrust
44	S	S	Right walking stance	Turn around & sit on the knee	Downward punch
45	S	S	Sit on the right knee	Move right foot a step forward	Wing spread
46-47	N E	N E	Left forward stance Right forward stance	Turn around & left downward block, Move over right foot	Left elbow target strike
48	N	NE	Right forward stance	right 'sword swallow'	Left high punch [shout of concentration]
49	N	N	Close stance	Move right foot around	Hammer fist target strike(8sec)
50	S	S	Right walking stance	Turn right foot around	Downward pushing block
51	N	N	Left forward stance	Turn left foot around	Right 'sword swallow' [shout of concentration]
Stop	N	N	Parallel stance	Pull in left foot	Basic ready stance

KTAA Poomsae V : 2nd Black Belt Poomsae

- Poomsae line:
- Recommended time : 71 Seconds
- Composition of Poomsae

The Geumgang Poomsae is composed monotonically with skills such as Geumgang-makgi(Diamond block), Santeul-makgi(Mountain block), Heheo-makgi(Double outward block), and Doljjeogwi(Hinge), etc. As for KTAA, hand techniques such as Batangson teokchigi (Palm hand chin strike), Pynson Santeul-makgi(Open hand Mountain block), and Utgeoreo-makgi(Wrist-crossed block) are added, and kicking techniques such as Ap-chagi(Front kick), Dollyeo-chagi(Roundhouse kick), and Dolgae-chagi(Turn kick) combined with Mulleo-ditgi(Backward step), Dora-ditgi (Turning step), and Yeop-ditgi(Side step) are supplemented. It is structured so that students can experience the intensity of the Geumgang Poomsae and the power of Taekwondo skills.

38　Modern Poomsae

KTAA Poomsae V : 2nd Black Belt Poomsae

KTAA Poomsae V : 2nd Black Belt Poomsae

Order	Eye direction	Body direction	Stance	Action	Name of pose
Ready	N	N	Parallel stance	One foot apart	Basic ready stance
1	W	N	Riding stance	Move left foot around	Left diamond downward block
2	W	W	Left forward stance	Slide left foot out slightly	Right middle punch
3	W	W	Right forward stance	Move right foot a step forward	Right chin strike
4	N	N	Riding stance	Move left foot around	Middle pushing block
5	E	N	Riding stance	While standing there	Right diamond downward block
6	E	E	Right forward stance	Slide right foot out slightly	Left middle punch
7	E	E	Left forward stance	Move left foot a step forward	Left chin strike
8-9-10	E / N	E / N	Left forward stance parallel stance	Right side kick & riding stance pushing block, pull in right foot	Downward pushing block(4sec)
11	NW	NW	Sparring stance	Move right foot a step backward	Sparring stance [shout of concentration]
12-13	NW	NW	Sparring stance	Drag the hind foot & roundhouse kick with the front foot	Right roundhouse kick
14-15	NW	NW	Sparring stance right forward stance	move a step backward & switch feet turn right foot around	right arm downward block and left fist middle punch at a time
16-17	NW / S	NW / S	Parallel stance	Right turn kick & turn around	Downward pushing block
18	E	E	Close stance Left forward stance	Cross wrists in front of chest moving right foot slightly & move left foot a step forward	Middle pushing block
19	E	E	Right forward stance	Move right foot a step forward & right palm hand chin strike	Left palm hand chin strike
20	E	E	Left forward stance	Move left foot a step forward	Right middle punch
21	E	N	Riding stance	Turn right foot around & take a step	Large hinge
22-23	N	N	Riding stance	Left 'hand knife' twisting outer block	Crossed 'hand knife' downward block
24-25	N	N	Right tiger stance	Pull in right foot & right single mountain block	Left single mountain block

40   Modern Poomsae

26	N	N	Riding stance	Trample with right foot	Mountain block [shout of concentration]
27	NE	NE	Right forward stance	Left foot cross over right foot & a step of right foot move forward	Assisted palm hand chin strike
28	SW	SW	Left forward stance	Turn left foot around	Downward pushing block
29	NW	NW	Riding stance	Move right foot a step forward & left foot a step forward	Crossed wrists mountain block
30-31	SW N N	SW N N	Left walking stance Tiger stance Riding stance	Move left foot a step forward & palm hand pressing block, turn right foot around & two 'hand knife' crossed block, slide left foot out slightly	Mountain block
32-33-34	E	N	Riding stance	Yoke punch & right large hinge, turn right	Left large hinge
35-36	NW NW	NW E	Left forward stance	Slide left foot out slightly & assisted right high punch	Right hammer fist downward strike
37	N	E	Riding stance	Move left foot around	Mountain block [shout of concentration]
38-39	N	N	Left tiger stance Parallel stance	Pull in left foot & middle pushing block, pull right foot to left foot	Downward pushing block(4sec)
40	W	N	Right crane stance	Pull left foot to right leg	Diamond downward block(8sec)
41-42-43	W	N	Riding stance	Left front kick & right large hinge, left foot turn around	Right large hinge
44	N	N	Right back stance	Move right foot a step backward	Left 'hand knife' inner block
45-46-47	N	N	Left back stance	Move left foot a step backward & right 'hand knife' inner block, right 'hand knife' high block	Lift left fist
48-49-50 -51-52 -53-54	E	N	Left crane stance Right forward stance Riding stance	Diamond downward block(4sec), lift right foot & front kick, a step forward & high punch twice, pull in right foot & double punch, move left foot slightly	Left large hinge [shout of concentration]
Stop	N	N	Parallel stance	Pull right foot next to left foot	Basic ready stance

KTAA Poomsae VI : 3rd Black Belt Poomsae

- Poomsae line:
- Recommended time : 69 Seconds
- Composition of Poomsae

Taebaek Poomsae consists of somewhat difficult but monotonous skills centered on two-handed blocking, punching, and striking techniques such as Hecheo-makgi(Double outward block), Gawi-makgi(Scissors block), Danggyeo -Jireugi(Pull and punch), and Jebipum-chigi(Swallow strike), etc. Therefore, the key techniques of Taebaek Poomsae are reconfigured in various ways by adding Nalgaepyogi(Two hands cleaving block), Hansonnal-mokchigi(one hand neck strike), and Hecho-makgi & Jeocheo-Jireugi(Double outward block & Turnover punch), etc. and by combining Narae-chagi(Double kick) and Dwi-chagi(Thrust kick) with Ap-chagi(Front kick), Dollyeo-chagi(Roundhouse kick), Mulleo-ditgi (Backward step), and Nae-ditgi(Forward step) to perform at moderate speed. KTAA Poomsae VI is designed so that students can experience the solidity of Taebaek Poomsae and the extraordinariness of Taekwondo skills.

shout of concentration

KTAA Poomsae VI : 3rd Black Belt Poomsae

KTAA Poomsae VI : 3rd Black Belt Poomsae

Order	Eye direction	Body direction	Stance	Action	Name of pose
Ready	N	N	Parallel stance	One foot apart	Basic ready stance
1-2 -3-4	N NW E	N NW E	Right forward stance Left forward stance	Move right foot & left 'hand knife' side strike, assisted 'sword swallow', right high block right knee bent	Left downward punch
5	W	W	Left tiger stance	Turn left foot around	'Hand knife' downward pushing block
6-7	W	W	Right forward stance	Right front kick & a step forward	Middle punch twice
8	E	E	Right tiger stance	Turn right foot around	Scissors block
9-10	E	E	Left forward stance	Left front kick & a step forward	Middle punch twice
11	N	N	Right back stance	Move left foot around	Diamond middle block
12	N	N	Left forward stance	Slide left foot out slightly	Swallow pose neck strike
13	N	N	Right forward stance	Move right foot a step forward & twist right wrist	Left middle punch
14	N	N	Left forward stance	Move left foot a step forward & twist left wrist	Right middle punch
15	N	N	Right forward stance	Move right foot a step forward & twist right wrist	Left middle punch [shout of concentration]
16	N	N	Right forward stance	Knees bent in place	Downward pushing block
17-18	N	N	Left crane stance	Cross block folding left knee	Wing spread
19	N	N	Right forward stance	Move left foot a step backward	Right middle punch
20	S	S	Right back stance	Turn left foot around	Left back-fist outer strike
21	S	S	Right back stance	Move right foot a step forward & left foot a step forward	Two 'hand knife' outer block
22	S	S	Right forward stance	Move right foot a step forward	Fingertip vertical thrust
23	S	N	Left back stance	Move left foot around	Remove the gripped wrist
24	W	N	Right tiger stance	Pull in left foot	Left 'hand knife' outer block(2sec)
25	N	N	Left back stance	Slide right foot out	Left chin-pulling strike(4sec)

26-27	N	N	Left back stance Right forward stance	Right middle punch(2sec) & slide right foot out	Middle punch twice
28	S	S	Sparring stance	Move left foot a step forward & step in place twice	Sparring stance [shout of concentration]
29-30 -31-32	N S	N S	sparring stance	Right roundhouse kick, left roundhouse kick, a step moves backward & double kick, turn around	Sparring stance [shout of concentration]
33-34 -35-36 -37-38	S S N	S S N	Sparring stance Left forward stance Riding stance	Step in place twice, left skipping kick & right back kick, a step backward & right roundhouse kick & left back kick, right middle punch & turn around	downward Downward pushing block
39	E	E	Left back stance	Twist right foot slightly	Two 'hand knife' outer block
40	E	E	Right forward stance	Move left foot a step forward	Diamond middle block
41-42 -43-44	E	E	Right back stance right crane stance	chin-pulling punch, left middle punch, right smaller hinge, left diamond side kick	Right elbow target strike
45	W	W	Right tiger stance	Turn right foot around	Left joint snapping
46-47	W	W	Left forwards stance Back cross stance	Move left foot a step forward & body pulling block	Turn-over punch
48	W	W	Right back stance	Move right foot a step backward	Two 'hand knife' outer block
49-50 -51-52 -53	W	W	Left back stance left crane stance right forward stance	Move right foot a step forward & diamond middle block, chin-pulling punch & right middle punch, pull right foot slightly & small hinge, right diamond side kick & put it down	left elbow target strike
54	N	N	Right tiger stance	Turn right foot around	'Hand knife' downward pushing block
Stop	N	N	Parallel stance	Pull in left foot	Basic ready stance

KTAA Poomsae VII : 4th Black Belt Poomsae

- Poomsae line: ⊥
- Recommended time : 71 Seconds
- Composition of Poomsae

Pyongwon Poomsae is designed to softly practice skills such as Palkup-ollyochigi(Elbow lift up strike), Olgul-kodure-Yopmakgi(Face assisting side block), Meongye-chigi(Yoke strike), and Hecho-santeulmakgi(Pushing mountain block), etc. KTAA Poomsae VII is designed to arrange hand techniques such as Sonnal-bakkatmakgi(Hand knife outward block), Sonal-Yeommakgi(Hand knife side block), and Sonal-naeryeomakgi(Hand knife downward block), etc. and foot techniques such as quick roundhouse, Huryeo-chagi(Whipping kick), and Nae-ditgi & Dwi-chagi(Forward step & thrust kick), etc. in the first half so that students can execute those skills very dynamically. And in the second half, the students can deeply experience the comparative meanings of passion and tranquility, threat and peace in the Pyongwon Poomsae while gently practicing the Poomsae.

50 Modern Poomsae

④ ⑧ ⑬ ㊼ ㊾
shout of concentration

KTAA Poomsae VII : 4th Black Belt Poomsae

KTAA Poomsae VII : 4th Black Belt Poomsae

Order	Eye direction	Body direction	Stance	Action	Name of pose
Ready	N	N	Parallel stance	One foot apart	Basic ready stance
1	N	N	Riding stance	Pull two fists & put them on the waist	Riding stance
2-3-4	N	N	Riding stance	Middle punch twice & high punch, right smaller hinge	Diamond punch [shout of concentration]
5-6 -7-8	N N N	NE NW N	Right forward stance Left forward stance Riding stance	Twist right foot slightly & left 'hand knife' downward block, right middle punch, Left elbow upward strike, left forward stance	Right high punch [shout of concentration]
9-10 -11-12	E W N N	N N N N	Left cross stance Right walking stance	Move left foot behind right foot & two 'hand knife' outer block, two 'hand knife' downward block & right 'hand knife' high block, left foot a step backward	Right 'hand knife' downward block(3sec)
13	N	N	Sparring stance	Move left foot a step backward	Sparring stance [shout of concentration]
14	N	N	Sparring stance	Step in place twice & switch step	Sparring stance
15-16 -17-18	N	N	Sparring stance	Left skipping kick, Right roundhouse kick, left spinning kick, right foot a step forward & left foot forward to make 'assisting stance'	Wing spread
19-20 21 22	N E	NW E	Left forward stance Right walking stance	Move left foot to the west & right 'hand knife' downward block, pull right foot & thrust downward with left fingertip at a time, move right foot a step backward & left back kick	Left arm downward block and right fist middle punch at a time
23-24	W	W	Parallel stance	Turn left foot around & right back spinning kick	Left downward block(4sec)
25-26-27	NE N N	NE N N	Right forward stance left cross stance riding stance	Move right foot a step forward & left joint snapping, move left foot around & back fist strike, move right foot around	Scissors block
28-29-30	E	E	Right walking stance Left tiger stance	Pull right foot slightly & right back fist strike, left target kick, take a step forward each with right and left foot	Left palm hand inner block
31	N	N	Riding stance	Move right foot a step forward	Mountain block

32	E	N	Left cross stance	Move left foot a step sideward	Yoke strike
33-34 -35-36 -37	N E W	N N W	Left cross stance Riding stance Left tiger stance	Crossed wrist upward block, move right foot sideward & crossed wrist downward block, right 'hand knife' side strike & left hight block, turn left & pull left foot	Right middle punch
38	W	W	Left forward stance	Slide left foot out	Right elbow upward strike
39-40-41	W	W	Sparring stance	Right front kick, left diamond side kick & move a step forward	Right elbow target strike
42	N	N	Left back stance	Pull right foot & move left foot a step backward	Two 'hand knife' outer block
43	N	N	Right back stance	Move right foot a step backward	Two 'hand knife' downward block
44-45	N	N	Right forward stance	Move left foot a step backward & right elbow upward strike	Left elbow chin strike
46	N	N	Riding stance	Pull right foot a step sideway	Assisted side block(2sec)
47-47-1	N	N	Riding stance	Trample with right foot & front strike with right back fist [shout of concentration]	Front strike supported by left back fist
48-49	E	N	Left cross stance	Move left foot sideway & yoke strike, move right foot sideway	Mountain block
50	E	E	Right forward stance	Move right foot sideway slightly	Left elbow upward strike
51-52-53	E W	E W	Right forward stance Right back stance	Left front kick, turn around & right side kick, turn around & two 'hand knife' outer block	Two 'hand knife' downward block(4sec)
54	W	W	Left forward stance	Slides left foot out slightly	Right middle punch
55-56	W	W	Right forward stance	Right side kick & put it down	Left elbow upward strike
57-58	W W	W W	Right foreard stance Riding stance	Move left foot a step forward & right palm hand chin strike, move right foot a step forward & move left foot a step sideway	Assisted side block(2sec)
59-59-1	N	N	Riding stance	Trample with left foot & left back fist assisted-front strike[shout of concentration]	Right back fist assisted-front strike
60-61	W	N	Right crane stance	Diamond downward block	Right smaller hinge
62-63	W	W	Right crane stance Left forward stance	Left back fist side strike Move left foot a step forward	Right high punch

Order	Eye direction	Body direction	Stance	Action	Name of pose
64-65	W E	W E	Right back stance	Right front kick & turn around and left side kick, two 'hand knife' outer block	Two 'hand knife' downward block
66	E	S	Riding stance	Move left foot a step sideway turning around	Mountain block
67-68	E	S	Right cross stance	Move right foot sideway & yoke strike, turn left foot around & move right foot a step forward	Right downward block(2sec)
Stop	N	N	Parallel stance	Pull left foot forward	Basic ready stance

● Introduction of Development Team •••

Cheontaik Son

RESUME

Ph. D., The Ohio State University
Professor, Incheon National University
Director, Taekwondo Research Institute of Kukkiwon
Director, Kukkiwon, World Taekwondo Headquarter
Acting president, Kukkiwon, World Taekwondo Headquarter
President, Korea Sport Pedagogy Association
President, Korea Taekwondo for All Association
Executive Director, Korea College Taekwondo Federation

Hyunchul Ji

Master, Korea National Sport University
Vice chairman, Grand Master Screening Committee
Senior vice chairman, Seoul Taekwondo Association Poomsae Division
International referee, World Takekwond Poomsae Division
Vice president, Korea Taekwondo for All Association
Director, Saeam Taekwond School
President, Kandong-Ku Taekwondo Associatin
Vice president, Global Newspaper

Sumin Ji

Master, Gachun University
Demonstration team, Seoul Sport for All Association
Coach, Kangdond-Ku Taekwondo Demonstration Team
Main instructor, Adidas Taekwondo Gymnastics
Captin, Arte Taekwondo Performance Team
Chairman, Korea Taekwondo for All Association Demonstration Team